*Law*Basics

GLOSSARY OF LEGAL TERMS

*Law*Basics

GLOSSARY OF LEGAL TERMS

FIFTH EDITION

By

Stephen R. O'Rourke

Advocate

W. GREEN **THOMSON REUTERS**

First Edition 1946 (Professor Dewar Gibb)
Reprinted 1971, 1975, 1978
Second Edition 1982 (A.G.M. Duncan)
Third Edition 1992 (A.G.M. Duncan)
Fourth Edition 2004 (Stephen R. O'Rourke)
Reprinted 2006

Published in 2009 by Thomson Reuters (Legal) Limited
(Registered in England & Wales, Company No 1679046.
Registered Office and address for service:
100 Avenue Road, London NW3 3PF
trading as W. Green)

Typeset by Keith Thaxton at W. Green, Edinburgh
Printed and bound in Great Britain by Athenaeum Press Ltd Gateshead

No natural forests were destroyed to make this product;
Only farmed timber was used and re-planted.

A CIP catalogue record for this book is available from the British Library.

ISBN 978 0 414 01753 5

Thomson Reuters and the Thomson Reuters logo are trademarks of
Thomson Reuters.

PREFACE TO THE FIFTH EDITION

It is just over five years since the last edition of the *Glossary*, at which time individual entries were extensively updated and revised. A significant number of new entries were added at that time. This time, however, there have been relatively fewer new additions. The list of reference books at the beginning has been extended and a list of useful websites has been added at the end. It is hoped that these additions will help the *Glossary* remain a concise and useful companion for anyone involved in or interested in Scots law.

Once again, my thanks to all the staff at W.Green for their assistance in producing this new edition.

April 2009   Stephen R. O'Rourke

PREFACE TO THE FOURTH EDITION

A.G.M. Duncan, who died in January 2003 aged 88, was the editor of the second and third editions of this book, in 1982 and 1992 respectively. Sadly he was unable to participate in the editing of this fourth edition as had been planned; though at a sprightly 88 there is no doubt in my mind that he would have been more than up to the task. Instead, this fourth edition is dedicated to him, a unique figure linking the old and the modern, the academic and practitioner, in legal education. He will be remembered affectionately by all who knew him, and his contribution to the law he loved will survive as long as there is a Scottish legal system.

The *Glossary* was last edited in 1992 and there have been a number of changes and additions to Scottish legal terminology since then. Principally, among other changes, this edition brings in terms following the introduction of the Scotland Act 1998, the Requirements of Writing (Scotland) Act 1995 and terms of EU law and the European Convention on Human Rights. Overall the aim of providing definitions for older and even obsolete terms of Scots law has been adhered to, in order to render assistance with those strange terms one often comes across in reading older court reports, court papers and textbooks.

The system of cross-referencing has been enhanced in order to assist understanding of how different definitions are linked. Cross-reference terms appear in bold, and italics have been used for Latin or foreign terms or maxims. The *Glossary* now also includes a brief list of acronyms at the end, principally relating to legal journals and official court reports.

In contradistinction to the stated aims of the first edition, more general and basic legal definitions have been added in order to widen the appeal of this text to lawyers and non-lawyers alike. It is hoped that the *Glossary* should be of use to anyone with a general interest or need to be familiar with Scottish legal terms of art.

Finally, my thanks for their patience and help in connection with the preparation and reproduction of the manuscript are due to the staff at W.Green, in particular to Valerie Malloch, Kathy Pauline and Louise Cardwell Miller; however the responsibility for such errors and omissions as remain is solely mine.

January 2004   Stephen R. O'Rourke

PREFACE TO THE THIRD EDITION

Ten years having elapsed since publication of the second edition of this manual, considerable updating has been necessary to reflect changes in law and practice. Basically, however, the format and content adopted by the late Professor Dewar Gibb in the First Edition has been retained although the length of the text now exceeds substantially that of the earlier editions. Since the publication of the Second Edition there have become available the late Mr John Beaton's *Scots Law Terms and Expressions* and the comprehensive glossary of legal terms and Latin phrases contained in the supplementary volume to the *Stair Memorial Encyclopedia*; both these publications and particularly the Stair glossary have been helpful in the preparation of this edition.

My thanks are due to Mr Ian Young and the other members of the staff at W.Green for their help in the reproduction of the manuscript. The responsibility of any errors and again for omissions almost inevitable in a work of this scope and diversity, must, however, be mine.

1992   A.G.M. DUNCAN

PREFACE TO THE SECOND EDITION

Since the publication of this *Glossary* in 1946, there have been many changes in the law which have been reflected in the introduction of new terms and have in some cases resulted in terms once in common usage becoming obsolete. This edition of Professor Dewar Gibb's work, which has been a valuable aid to successive generations of law students, attempts, without departing from its basic framework or materially extending its scope, to adapt it to meet the requirements of those embarking today on the study of the law, whether with a view to professional qualification or as part of a course of study for some other calling. Unfortunate as it may be from the point of view of the budding legal historian, this has necessitated the exclusion of a substantial number of items which the author had himself described as obsolete and of other terms which appear to have lost their practical significance. In this way, space has been made for the inclusion of new terms and for some amplification in the adaptation of certain parts of the original text. Again, some additions have been made to the Latin terms included which it was felt might be helpful with works such as Trayner and Connolly and Brown out of print and not always readily available to students. Inevitably, however, given the scope of the work, no attempt has been made to cover the terminology of specialized fields such as rent control or consumer protection or other such areas of modern development.

Professor Dewar Gibb included in the text against certain items only, references to authorities such as institutional writers. It is not always clear why particular items have been singled out for this treatment and again some of the sources referred to may not be easily reached. To provide such references throughout the glossary would have added considerably to its content and in the circumstances it has been thought better to omit all such references from the text but to provide a separate list of books which should be available to most users of the glossary in libraries or otherwise. In this connection particular mention should be made of Professor D.M. Walker's *Oxford Companion to Law*, a comprehensive source of information about law and related matters.

Brief definitions of legal terms are sometimes impossible without the use of other terms which may not be self-explanatory. In some cases but not in others, Professor Dewar Gibb used the insertion "q.v." to indicate a term to be found elsewhere in the glossary. In this edition it has been thought better to omit this form of cross-referencing but it will be found that where legal terms have been used in defining others the former will generally be appearing in their alphabetical places in the glossary.

My thanks for their patience and help in connection with the preparation and reproduction of this manuscript are due to the General Manager of W.Green & Sons Ltd., Miss Iris Stewart, and her staff, and particularly to the Legal Editor, Mr Peter Nicholson, who read the proofs and made a number of helpful suggestions. The responsibility for such errors and omissions as remain, is, however, mine.

May 1982   A.G.M. DUNCAN

INTRODUCTION TO THE FIRST EDITION

In every legal system there are terms of art which must necessarily puzzle the layman. Included in the term layman is the young man beginning the study of law. It is too often taken for granted by those who instruct him that the student knows the meaning of the curious words and expressions which are part of the teacher's normal vocabulary. That however is far from being the case, and as a result a good many lawyers go through life with a hazy or even a wrong idea of the sense of certain expressions. What meaning for example could the novice take out of the statement in a students' text-book that "the only passive title in moveables is vitious intromission," without a previous explanation of "passive title"?

Perhaps this little book, based on recognised authorities, and written, it is hoped, in reasonably intelligible terms, may go some way towards improving that state of matters. It may be too that others than students who have to wrestle with the meaning of the voces signatae of Scots law will find it useful.

The book is concerned almost exclusively with legal expressions which are truly and exclusively lawyers' expressions. It does not purport to explain words which are part of lay language and reasonably well understood, such as "contract," "murder," "condition" and the like. Thus delimited, the collection consists mainly of words peculiar to Scots law or which have a particular meaning attached to them by Scots law. The separation of lawyer's and layman's language in Scotland is the more acute because a Scots lawyer may have a technical term for the expression of some idea which the layman usually expresses by an English word that is at once a lawyer's and a layman's word. Thus a Scottish layman uses the word "bankruptcy" which is the English popular and technical word. Few Scots laymen would use "sequestration" which, however, is the correct legal expression for bankruptcy in Scotland. Again, for every Scotsman who speaks of "confirmation," there are ten who will use "probate".

The Scottish legal vocabulary is interesting and fairly extensive. It has a number of components which vary in quality and origin. Thus there is the English term (legal or lay) with a special meaning, like "embezzle." There is the word drawn from the Scottish language, like "thole" or the Scots variant of an English term, like "assignation". There is also a class of words which, so to speak simulate English words but which are simply unknown in English or at least in modern English; for example "approbate" or "stellionate." It is the vocabulary consisting of all these classes of words and expressions that is to be found in this Glossary.

September 1946   A.D.G.

CONTENTS

BOOKS OF REFERENCE

General Reference
- Bates, T.St. J.N. and Paterson, A.A., *The Legal System of Scotland*, 4th edn (Edinburgh: W. Green, 1999)
- Gloag & Henderson, *The Law of Scotland*, 12th edn (Edinburgh: W. Green, 2007)
- Marshall, Enid A., *General Principles of Scots Law*, 7th edn (Edinburgh: W. Green, 1999)
- Walker, D.M., *The Oxford Companion to Law* (Oxford: Oxford University Press, 1980)
- Walker, D.M., *The Scottish Legal System*, 8th edn (Edinburgh: W. Green, 2001)
- Walker, D.M., *Principles of Scottish Private Law*, 4th edn (Oxford: Clarendon Press, 1988)
- Wilson, W.A., *Introductory Essays on Scots Law* (Edinburgh: W. Green, 1978)
- *The Encyclopaedia of the Laws of Scotland* (15 volumes) (Edinburgh: W.Green, 1926–1952) (Note: While not supplemented since 1952, this work remains a valuable source of information on many topics)
- *The Laws of Scotland: Stair Memorial Encyclopaedia* (25 volumes) (Scotland: Butterworths, 1991)
- *The Scottish Legal Tradition*, new enlarged edition by Lord Cooper, W.D.H. Sellar and M.C. Meston (Edinburgh: Saltire Society, 1991)

On Court Procedure
- Welsh, T., *Macphail's Sheriff Court Practice*, 3rd edn, 2 vols (Edinburgh: W. Green, 2006)
- Maxwell, D., *The Practice of the Court of Session* (Scottish Courts Administration, 1980)
- *Court of Session Practice* (Sussex: Tottel)

On Criminal Law
- Gordon, G.H., *The Criminal Law of Scotland*, 3rd edn, 2 vols (Edinburgh: W. Green, 2005)
- Jones, T.H. and Christie, M.G.A., *Criminal Law*, 4th edn (Edinburgh: W.Green, 2008)

On Conveyancing and Land Law
- Gordon, W.M., *Scottish Land Law*, 2nd edn (Edinburgh: W. Green, 1999)
- Gretton, G.L. & Reid, K.G.C., *Conveyancing*, 3rd edn (Edinburgh: W. Green, 2004)
- Halliday, J.M., *Conveyancing Law and Practice in Scotland*, 2nd edn, 2 vols (Edinburgh: W. Green, 1996–1997)

On the Law of Succession
- Macdonald, D.R., *Succession*, 3rd edn (Edinburgh: W. Green, 2001)

On the Law of Contract
- McBryde, W.W., *The Law of Contract in Scotland*, 3rd edn (Edinburgh: W. Green, 2007)
- Woolman, S. and Lake, J., *Contract*, 3rd edn (Edinburgh: W.Green, 2001)

On Company Law
- Grier, N., *Company Law*, 2nd edn (Edinburgh: W. Green, 2005)

On the Law of Evidence
- Raitt, F., *Evidence: Principles, Policy & Practice*, 4th edn (Edinburgh: W. Green, 2008)

On Constitutional and Public Law
- Ashton, C. and Finch, V., *Constitutional Law in Scotland*, (Edinburgh: W. Green, 2000)
- Munro, J., *Public Law*, 2nd edn (Edinburgh: W. Green, 2007)

On Family Law
- Edwards, L. and Griffiths, A., *Family Law*, 2nd edn (Edinburgh: W. Green, 2006)

On International Private Law
- Crawford, E.B. and Carruthers, J.M., *International Private Law in Scotland*, 2nd edn (Edinburgh: W. Green, 2006)

On Legal History
- Reid, K. and Zimmermann, R., *A History of Private Law in Scotland*, 2 vols (Oxford: Oxford University Press, 2000)

Latin Terms and Phrases
- Trayner, J., *Latin Maxims and Phrases*, 4th edn (Edinburgh: W. Green, 1894)
- Connolly, T.J.D., *Select Scots Law Maxims* (Edinburgh: W. Green, 1934)

A

A caelo usque ad centrum.

Literally, from the heavens to the centre (of the earth). The term is used in feudal law to indicate ownership of land itself and everything directly underneath and above. Such ownership is qualified, e.g. by reservation of mineral rights underground, or by statute in order to allow aeroplane flightpaths over private property.

Abbreviate.

(i) Of adjudication; an abstract of a decree of adjudication containing the names of debtor and creditor, the lands adjudged and the amount of the debt registered as a necessary step in the process of adjudication. See **Adjudication**.

(ii) In **bankruptcy**; an abbreviate or abstract of the petition for sequestration and the first deliverance must be registered. Other abbreviates are known in bankruptcy proceedings.

Absolute bar.

In the **European Court of Justice**, a ground for the refusal of consideration of the merits of an action.

Absolute exclusivity.

The quality of an agreement (such as a licence or assignation of an industrial, commercial or intellectual property right) by which A agrees:

(i) to supply goods for resale in a particular geographical area to B and to no other person;

(ii) not to compete with B in that area; and

(iii) to prevent other persons from competing with B. See **Open exclusivity**.

Absolvitor.

A court decree in a civil action, in favour of the defender. Decree of absolvitor renders a case **res judicata**. When a defender obtains decree of absolvitor he is said to be **assoilzied**. Absolvitor contrasts with decree of dismissal, which does not render a case **res judicata** and accordingly allows a pursuer to bring a fresh action on the same grounds.

Abstract.

A summary or precis of a document.

Acceptilation.

Extinction of debt by an arrangement which falls short of full performance.

Access.

(i) In family law the right, sometimes requiring court regulation, of one parent to visit, meet, or be with a child under 16 who is in the custody of the other parent. Also referred to as **Contact**.

(ii) In property law a means of reaching one's property that can involve traversing the property of another.

Accession.

(i) Natural or artificial addition to existing things whereby additional property is acquired, as, e.g. the young of animals, or a new house built on one's land. See *Alluvio*; *Avulsio*.

(ii) The admission to the European Union of a state other than a founding member.

Accession, deed of.

A deed executed by the creditors of an insolvent, approving and accepting an arrangement by him for settling his affairs.

Accessory.

Primarily a term of English law, it is a person who aids in some way the perpetration of a crime. See **Art and part**.

Accessory action.

An action that subserves a higher legal purpose as, e.g. proving of the tenor, in order later to base a claim upon the deed set up by the action.

Accessory obligation.

An obligation following logically from an earlier principal obligation, e.g. the obligation to pay interest is an accessory to the obligation to repay the sum on which the interest is accruing.

Account of charge and discharge.

An account, usually annual, of the transactions of factors, executors, trustees and the like, or their agents, with the property committed to their care.

Accountant in Bankruptcy.

The Accountant of Court in his capacity as administrative supervisor of sequestrations and personal insolvency. See **Accountant of Court**.

Accountant of Court.

An officer of court who supervises the conduct of judicial factors, curators, tutors, guardians and others appointed by the Court of Session or Sheriff Court. He also carries out the functions of the **Accountant in Bankruptcy**.

Accretion.

(i) When the imperfect title of A, who has conveyed to B, is later perfected in A, this validation "accresces" to and perfects B's title.

(ii) Occurs in the case of joint legatees when one dies and his share goes or accrues to the others.

(iii) The means by which joint property is transferred.

Accused.

A person charged with committing a crime or offence. See **Panel**.

Acquiescence.

A form of personal bar arising from a person's failure to object timeously to an infringement of his rights, or the tacit acceptance of a particular course of conduct or state of affairs.

Act and warrant.

The **interlocutor** in sequestration proceedings which confirms the appointment of the trustee.

Actings.

A favourite but unnecessary synonym for "acts" or "conduct".

Action.

Proceedings instituted by a person in a civil court. The person initiating a civil action in Scotland is termed the pursuer. The person against whom the action is raised is termed the defender. On appeal in civil matters, the party appealing is termed the appellant while the other is termed the respondent. This is so irrespective of whether the party appealing was originally the pursuer or the defender.

Acts of Adjournal.

Regulations as to procedure made by the High Court of Justiciary in virtue of statutory power.

Act of God.

See *damnum fatale*.

Acts of Sederunt.

Procedural rules made by the judges of the Court of Session in virtue of statutory power.

Acts of the Scottish Parliament.

Devolved legislation passed by the **Scottish Parliament** since 1999, as distinct from **Scottish Acts of Parliament** which is legislation of the old Scottish parliament prior to the Treaty of Union in 1707.

Ad factum praestandum.

An obligation or an order of court to perform an act other than the payment of money. See **Specific implement**.

Adhere.

This word means:

(i) of husband or wife, to remain with and be faithful (to the other); and

(ii) of a court, to affirm the judgment of a lower court.

Ad hoc.

Referring only to a particular case or to a specified set of circumstances.

Ad interim.

In the meantime.

Adjudication.

(i) A form of diligence used to attach heritable property. Adjudication is obtained by way of an action of adjudication in the Court of Session. The effect of a recording of an extract decree of adjudication in the Register of Sasines or in the Land Register has the effect of a heritable security in favour of the adjudicating creditor. If the debt remains unsatisfied after a period of 10 years (known as the "legal"), the adjudger may acquire ownership by taking decree in an action of declarator of the expiry of the legal. See **Inhibition; Arrestment and furthcoming; Attachment**.

(ii) The decision of the Commissioners of Inland Revenue as to the stamp duty payable on a deed or instrument.

(iii) In the United Kingdom, a legal process for the resolution of disputes in the construction industry. Adjudication is provided for by the Housing Grants, Construction and Regeneration Act 1996. The decision of the adjudicator, appointed to resolve the dispute, is enforceable through the Courts.

Adjust.

To alter the averments or pleas in a written pleading, before the record is closed. See **Amend**.

Ad litem.

As regards an action. See, e.g. *curator ad litem*.

Ad longum.

At length or in full.

Adminicle.

A piece of supporting or corroborative evidence.

Administration order.

A court order appointing an administrator for a company in financial difficulties but not hopelessly insolvent.

Administrator in law.

A title given to a father or to a mother in his or her relationship to children who are under 16.

Adoption.

(i) The statutory process whereby the parental rights and duties of natural parents are extinguished and vested in adopters.

(ii) The acceptance as valid of a transaction or contract, deed or document otherwise defective in some respect, e.g. acceptance of liability by a party whose signature on a bill has been forged.

Ad valorem.

According to value; e.g. the computation of Stamp Duty on a deed or document.

Advise.

To advise is to give a considered judgment in a case. See *Avizandum*.

Advocate.

(i) A member of the Scottish Bar; also a solicitor who is a member of the Society of Advocates in Aberdeen. And see **Lord Advocate**.

(ii) As a verb, to bring up the judgment of an inferior court for review—now incompetent in civil cases: in criminal cases rare but still competent as confirmed in recent legislation.

4

(iii) To apply to a superior court for review of a judgement of an inferior court. The process, which is referred to as a Bill of Advocation, is restricted to criminal jurisdiction. See **Suspension**.

Advocate Depute.

An advocate, solicitor advocate or procurator fiscal appointed by the Lord Advocate to prosecute in the High Court of Justiciary under his directions, and paid by salary. There are presently three levels of seniority: Senior Advocate Depute; Advocate Depute and Ad Hoc Advocate Depute. The Lord Advocate and the Solicitor General together with the Advocate Deputes are collectively referred to as **Crown Counsel**.

Advocate General.

An impartial judicial officer of the **European Court of Justice** to whom a pending case is assigned. The Advocate General attends the court's hearings and provides oral submissions recommending solutions to the issues of fact and law.

Advocate General for Scotland.

Following devolution, the Advocate General for Scotland replaces the Lord Advocate and the Solicitor General for Scotland as sole advisor to the UK government on Scots law. The Advocate General for Scotland is a Minister of the Crown and one of the three UK **Law Officers**, the others being the Attorney General and the Solicitor General for England and Wales.

Advocate, Lord.

One of the two Scottish Law Officers, the other being the **Solicitor General**. Following devolution, the Lord Advocate is a member of the **Scottish Executive** appointed by the Queen on the recommendation of the **First Minister**, together with the agreement of the **Scottish Parliament** (of which the Lord Advocate can, but need not, be a member). He is the Scottish Executive's chief legal adviser. As head of Crown Office he is independently responsible for ordering investigations of crimes, bringing public prosecutions in Scotland's courts, and ordering investigations of deaths. Prior to devolution, the Lord Advocate (together with the **Solicitor General**) advised the UK government on Scots law; this is now the function of the **Advocate General for Scotland**. See **Procurator fiscal**.

Aemulatio vicini.

Spite against one's neighbour that, if a motive, may render unlawful an act that is normally within a person's legal power.

Affidavit

A signed statement made on oath as used in undefended divorce proceedings and in property transactions affected by the Matrimonial Homes (Family Protection) (Scotland) Act 1981. Generally any written statement made on oath and signed.

Agent.

In its formal sense signifies a person acting on behalf of another, his principal. In proceedings before the **European Court of Justice**, the representative of a member state. See **Law agent**.

Aggravation.

Some circumstance in a criminal charge, as, e.g. a previous conviction, which, if proved, renders conviction more serious.

Agnate.

Agnates are persons related through the father. See **Cognate**.

Agricultural holding.

A farm let on a tenancy subject to the Agricultural Holdings legislation.

Aliment.

Support or maintenance of a wife or relative enforceable by law. The word is also used as a verb.

Alimentary.

Of the nature of or by way of ailment, as a fund or payment. The word connotes freedom from the claims of creditors.

Allenarly.

Only, merely. Important when associated with a **liferent** as preventing the liferent from being construed as a fee.

Allodial.

Non-feudal, as applied to the tenure of land, as in the case of udal tenure and church property.

Allotment.

(i) A small area of ground let by a local authority for cultivation by the occupier.

(ii) The appropriation of shares in a company to applicants.

Alluvio (or Alluvion).

Gradual accretion to land caused by the action of a river. The owner of the land that is increased, benefits. See *Avulsio*.

Altius non tollendi.

See **Light and prospect**.

Amend.

To alter with the sanction of the court the instance, conclusion or crave in an action, or after the record is closed the averments or pleas in law. See **Adjust**.

Annual rent.

Interest on money lent. So called because when—before the Reformation—interest was illegal, a sum derived from land was made payable by way of evasion.

Annuity.

The right to a yearly payment in money.

Answer.

A written pleading given in to a court usually in reply to a claim.

Apocha trium annorum.

Literally, a receipt of three years: three successive periodic payments, raising a presumption of payment of earlier instalments.

Apparent.

See **Heir**.

Apparent insolvency.

The circumstances replacing by statute the concept of **notour bankruptcy**, as a pre-requisite of the initiation by creditors of proceedings for sequestration. Apparent insolvency can arise in a number of ways, but is in any event the first stage of bankruptcy. The phrase "notour bankruptcy" was originally used to describe the condition of a man who, to avoid imprisonment for debt, had retired to the sanctuary of the Abbey of Holyrood, his insolvency thereby becoming notorious or "notour". See also **Insolvency; Sequestration**.

Appearance.

The formal act whereby the defender in an action intimates his intention to defend within three days of the calling of the **Summons**.

Appoint.

To order, or direct, as of a court.

Apportion.

To separate or divide as in the case of trust funds between income and capital or **liferent** and fee, or in the case of rents of property between seller and purchaser.

Appraiser.

The person appointed to value goods that were the subject of a poinding. See **Poind**.

Apprehend, to.

The true Scottish term of art for "to arrest" in a criminal sense.

Approbate and reprobate.

Approve, accept or adopt, and disapprove, refuse or reject respectively. It is commonly said that a deed or transaction cannot be approbated and reprobated, i.e. that a party must elect to accept all or reject all.

Apud acta.

Literally, at the time of the proceedings; notice of future proceedings is given *apud acta* when it is given orally at a sitting of the court without written citation. A rare expression.

Aquaeductus (or **Aqueduct**).

A servitude right to convey water by pipes or canals through the property of the servient owner. See **Servitude**.

Aquaehaustus.

A servitude under which the servient owner must permit watering cattle or taking water at his ponds or wells. See **Servitude**.

Arbiter (in England: **Arbitrator**).

A person chosen or appointed to decide in a dispute between parties.

Arles. (pr. "arr-ols")

Also referred to as "Earnest", is a small sum of money or part of a larger quantity given as a symbol or token of the completion of a bargain.

Arrestment and furthcoming.

Arrestment and furthcoming are the two stages of one form of diligence; and furthcoming is not competent without arrestment. Arrestment involves the seizing of a debtor's moveable property ("the arrestee") in the custody of a third party ("the common debtor"), thus personally preventing the third party disposing of the arrestee's property. Arrestment is then followed by an action of furthcoming brought against the arrestee and common debtor, in which the common debtor is ordained to pay the debt directly to the arresting creditor. Alternatively the property arrested is sold and the proceeds paid over. See **Adjudication; Inhibition; Attachment**.

Art and part.

Where a group of individuals act together for a common criminal purpose, they are each responsible "art and part" for that which any one member of the group does in furtherance of that common purpose. Guilt "art and part" is an exception to the general principle that a person is normally only responsible for his own actings.

Article.

A clause, paragraph or section of a legal document.

Articles of Association.

Regulations for the management of a company registered under the Companies Acts. See **Memorandum of Association**.

Articles of roup.

See **Roup**.

Artificial person (otherwise juristic person).

An entity such as a company to which personality is attributed by law.

As accords of law.

As is agreeable or conformable to law. Often shortened to "as accords".

Ascendant.

In a question of succession, a person akin to the deceased in a preceding generation, e.g. a parent, uncle or aunt.

Assedation.

A lease.

Assessor.

(i) A person with specialised knowledge relevant to the subject matter of a litigation who assists the judge or judges to reach a decision.

(ii) In local government, a person who assesses the annual value of properties where relevant for rating purposes.

Assignation (in England: **Assignment**).

The transfer of a right (e.g. to pursue a money debt or the tenancy of a lease) from one party (the cedent) to another (the assignee); an assigning of a right or rights (as formerly of rents or writs in a disposition): or, the instrument by which a right is assigned.

Assize.

In Scotland this word is occasionally and formally used to mean a jury. It also used to mean the sittings of a court.

Associate.

In the law of bankruptcy and insolvency, a person within certain categories of relationship with a bankrupt or insolvent person.

Assoilzie. (pr."ah-soil-lay")

To absolve or decide finally in favour of a defender. Where a defender obtains a decree of absolvitor he is said to be "assoilzied".

Assume.

To adopt, as of a new trustee or partner.

Assythment. (pr. "ahs-eye-th-ment")

Solatium or indemnification that could at one time be claimed by the relatives of a person whose death resulted from a criminal act. A statutory provision has made the claim incompetent now.

Attachment.

A form of diligence created by statute over corporeal moveable property for the recovery of a money debt. Items subject to Attachment are subsequently publicly auctioned. Attachment is the statutory replacement for poinding. See **Adjudication; Arrestment and furthcoming; Inhibition**.

Attestation.

The authentication of a deed or instrument by the signature (with designation) of the witness before whom it was signed or to whom the signatory declared his signature. See **Testing clause**.

Attorney.

A person acting under the authority of a **Power of attorney**. In England, but not in Scotland, the term is applied to solicitors in general as agents of their clients. See **Factory**.

Attour.

Besides, over and above.

Auctor in rem suam.
Agent for his own advantage; a role which neither agent nor trustee is allowed to assume.

Auditor.
A person charged with the duty of examining accounts. The Auditors of the Court of Session and Sheriff Court respectively examine and are said to "tax" accounts of expenses incurred in the respective courts. Cf. in England the taxing-master.

Audit Scotland.
The auditing body presided over by the **Auditor General for Scotland**.

Auditor General for Scotland.
An individual responsible for securing the audit of the **Scottish Executive** and most other public bodies in Scotland, except local authorities. The Auditor's task is to investigate (through **Audit Scotland**) whether spending bodies achieve the best possible value for money and adhere to the highest standards of financial management. Appointed by the Crown, the Auditor is independent of the **Scottish Executive** and **Scottish Parliament**. The Auditor's reports are laid before the Scottish Parliament, normally for the consideration of the parliament's Audit Committee.

Augmentation.
An increase in the amount of a periodical payment such as feuduty, stipend or rent.

Authentication.
The features of a deed or instrument establishing its genuineness or validity, e.g. the **attestation**.

Author.
One from whom a person derives a title, e.g. by sale or gift.

Authority.
The warrant or justification for a proposition or statement of the law in a particular matter, e.g. a statute, a precedent represented by a decided case or a statement of an institutional writer.

Aver.
To state or allege, particularly in written pleadings.

Avizandum.
Originally *avizandum est* in full, the single word *avizandum* is used as a noun and the court "makes *avizandum*" when it rises and takes time to consider its judgment. Cf. the English, *curia advisari vult* meaning "the court wishes to advise".

Avulsio.
A sudden and obvious addition to land by the action of a river or the sea, Unlike *alluvio*, it causes no change of property.

Award.
A decision in favour of a party to a dispute sometimes applied to a court's ruling but more commonly to that of a **tribunal** or **arbiter**.

B

Back (or Back up).
(i) Where legal documents are traditionally folded in half lengthways, to write on the back of the folded document details, e.g. names of parties, the type of deed, the date, etc.
(ii) To endorse a warrant in order to permit its execution outwith the original jurisdiction.

Back-bond (or **Back letter**).
An instrument that qualifies some other instrument that is in unqualified terms.

Backhand rent.
Rent payable in arrears, i.e. at the end of each period of the lease. See **Forehand rent**.

Bad faith.
In bad faith or *mala fide*, i.e. lacking good faith; applying, e.g. to a possessor of property on a title which he knows or has reasonable grounds to know is bad. See **Good faith**.

Bail.
In criminal proceedings an arrangement for the release of an accused person pending trial formerly requiring a deposit of money subject to forfeiture but under recent statutory provisions replaced in most cases by a conditional release subject to penalties. See **Caution**.

Baillie.
A magistrate in a Scottish burgh as constituted before the reorganisation of local government in 1975.

Bairns' part of gear.
See *Legitim*.

Bankrupt.
In common usage employed to describe three situations, namely **Insolvency; Apparent insolvency; Sequestration**.

Bankruptcy.
See **Apparent insolvency**.

Bar.
(i) In criminal proceedings the plea in bar of trial seeks to prevent the proceedings continuing on the ground, e.g. of insanity on the part of the accused or want of jurisdiction in the court.
(ii) In civil matters, see **Personal bar**.

(iii) The collective term for members of the Faculty of Advocates in Scotland, being persons "called to the bar", who are entitled to represent litigants in the highest courts.

Barony.

An estate in land created by direct grant from the Crown constituting a freehold barony. The resultant privileges in the form of civil and criminal jurisdiction have been abolished but certain special rights such as the possibility of acquisition of *regalia minora* (e.g. salmon fishings) by prescription survive.

Base holding.

A holding from one not the original superior of a feudal holding. When A feus land to B and B sub-feus to X, the right of X is base.

Before answer.

Before the law of a case is decided. Thus when a proof is allowed "before answer", the facts are brought out, but the legal argument that they do not entitle the person to relief is still competent.

Beneficiary.

A person entitled to some benefit under a will or trust.

Beneficium.

A privilege, benefit or right, e.g. as in the expression *beneficium ordinis*, the right of discussion of a cautioner at common law (now abolished); and *beneficium divisionis*, the right of a cautioner that a co-cautioner share the obligation **pro rata**.

Bill.

(i) A form of procedure in the Court of Session largely obsolete but nominally competent in certain cases; see **Exceptions; Suspensions**.

(ii) A form of document constituting a debt or pecuniary obligation, e.g. a bill of exchange.

(iii) A set of provisions submitted to the Westminster Parliament or **Scottish Parliament** that if passed will become an Act or statute.

Bill Chamber.

A court forming part of the Court of Session dealing with certain special matters including proceedings initiated by bills. Since 1933 its place has been taken by the Petition Department.

Blackmail.

From "maills" meaning "rent", originally a payment exacted from landowners by robbers for exemption from their raids, i.e. a form of protection money, hence "blackmail" now applied to illegal extortion generally.

Blank, Bonds in.

Bonds in which the creditor's name was left blank and which "passed from hand to hand like notes payable to the bearer." They were rendered null by the Act 1696, c.25, as facilitating fraud.

Blench (or less commonly **Blanch**).

An epithet (used also adverbially) descriptive of a feudal holding where the *reddendo* (i.e. feuduty or other services) is merely nominal, e.g. a rose.

Blench-ferme, Charter of.

The deed by which the feudal tenure of "Blench" or "Blenche-ferme" was established. See **Blench**.

Blood relationship.

The relationship existing between two persons having at least one common parent, the relationship being of the full blood when both parents are the same and of the half blood where only one parent is common. See **Consanguinean; Uterine**.

Bona fide ("in good faith"); **Bona fides** ("good faith").

See **Good faith**.

Bona vacantia.

Property of person dying without successors that falls to the Crown.

Bond.

A written obligation to pay money or to do some act. Until the introduction in 1970 of the standard security the "bond and disposition in security" was the normal statutory form constituting a debt secured by the debtor's heritable property. See also **Caution; Corroboration**.

Bonded warehouse.

Premises licensed by the Commissioners of Customs and Excise for the storage of excisable goods on which duty has still to be paid.

Booking.

A mode of landholding, peculiar to the Burgh of Paisley, in which a disponee secured a real right not by infeftment but by booking or registration in a Register of Booking, at one time after formal proceedings in the Council Chamber. Since the Registrar of Booking was terminated in 1927 and Registration therein replaced by registration in the General Register of Sasines the distinction between this and ordinary feudal tenure has in effect disappeared.

Books of Adjournal.

The books or records of the Justiciary Court.

Books of Council and Session.

A popular title for the Registers of Deeds and Probative Writs in which, according to the directions they contain, deeds, etc., may be registered for preservation or preservation and execution.

Books of Sederunt.

Records of the **Acts of Sederunt** in the Court of Session.

Border warrant.

A warrant for the arrest of the effects and person of someone in England for debts owed in Scotland: now obsolete.

Bounding charter (or **title**).

One that defines the land comprised in it by description of the boundaries thus excluding the possibility of expansion or enlargement by possession and prescription.

Bowing.

Mainly in Ayreshire and Galloway, a contract by which A lets out his herd to X (the bower) to be grazed on A's farm. The bower retains the profit, e.g. from a dairy herd, the milk.

Box.

A term formerly used for the lodging of papers at the commencement of proceedings in the Court of Session.

Brevi manu.

Directly, or by short cut. *Brevi manu* action is action taken to redress a legal wrong without the interposition of the court.

Brieve (also **Breve**).

A warrant from Chancery authorising an inquest or inquiry by a jury into any one of a variety of questions, such as the appointment of a tutor to a pupil or a curator to an insane person. Now practically obsolete being superseded by procedure by petition.

Brocard.

A term for a legal maxim derived from Roman law or ancient custom, e.g. caveat emptor—let the buyer take care.

Burden.

(i) In property law a limitation, restriction or encumbrance affecting land.

(ii) In court procedure—burden of proof. See **Onus**.

Burgage.

Burgage tenure was the type of holding under which property in royal burghs was held of the Crown. It is now obsolete as a separate tenure and registration of deeds in the burgh registers has been replaced by registration in the General Register of Sasines.

Burgh.

A Scottish town whose inhabitants were incorporated by Royal Charter or by statute. Since 1975 burghs have ceased to have distinct local government functions being absorbed in local authority districts with district courts replacing burgh courts.

Burrows.

See **Lawburrows**.

Bye-laws.

(i) A form of subordinate legislation by a body such as a local authority under powers delegated by Parliament.

(ii) Rules of internal management made by the council or committee of a body such as a club or society in exercise of powers contained in the constitution.

C

Caduciary.

Subject to lapse, forfeiture or confiscation. Rare.

Call.

(i) In the Court of Session a summons is called by the exhibition in a list on a wall of the court, of the names of parties and the legal representatives of the pursuer. From the calling date is reckoned the time for entering appearance.

(ii) In company law a call is a demand by the company or its liquidators for payments by shareholders with shares not fully paid.

(iii) In written pleadings, a request by one party that another make a specific averment within their knowledge.

Calumny, Oath of.

An oath taken at the outset of an action to the effect that the facts pleaded are believed true. For long obsolete except in consistorial cases in which, until 1977, it was required of pursuers.

Candlemas.

One of the four quarter days in Scotland, the others being Lammas, Martinmas and Whitsunday. Candlemas was formerly the second day of February but now by statute is the 28th day of that month. See **Whitsunday; Martinmas; Lammas**.

Capax.

In law, able to act and give legal instructions. See *Incapax*.

Capita, Succession per.

See **Per capita**.

Caption, letters of.

Formerly a bill chamber application to the Court of Session for the arrest and imprisonment of a civil debtor, a Bill of Letters of Caption would follow a Bill of Letters for Horning. Having been "put to the horn" and denounced, the debtor by virtue of Letters of Caption could then be imprisoned for his civil debt. See **Horning** and separately **Process Caption**.

Case or cause.

The action or proceedings in a civil court.

Case law.

Judicial decisions as a source of law.

Cash credit.

An arrangement for a loan whereby the borrower on giving security may draw, up to a limit, what he needs and may repay from time to time, paying interest only on what he actually takes out. The loan if secured over heritable property was formerly constituted by a bond of cash credit and disposition in security but since 1970 this has been superseded by a standard security.

Casual homicide.

An accidental killing involving no fault in the killer.

Casualty.

A payment falling due to a superior or landlord on the happening of events of uncertain date or occurrence. Now abolished in feus and disallowed in leases entered into since September 1, 1974.

Casus amissionis.

The occasion or circumstance of a loss; in particular, the manner in which a writing was lost must be established in an action of proving the tenor.

Casus improvisus.

A situation or contingency not foreseen or not provided for.

Casus omissus.

A case or situation omitted or not provided for, e.g. in a statute where the omission will as a general rule be regarded as intentional.

Catholic creditor.

One who holds security for his debt over more than one piece of property belonging to his debtor. See **Secondary creditor**.

Causa causans.

The immediate cause; the proximate or direct cause of some loss or damage sustained. See *Causa sine qua non*.

Causa sine qua non.

In the law of causation, the cause but for which some loss or damage sustained would not have occurred. The *causa sine qua non* can but need not be the immediate cause, i.e. the *causa causans*.

Cautio usufructuaria.

Caution obtained by the fiar from the liferenter to serve as security until termination of the **liferent**. The *cautio* is provided for under the old Scots Acts of 1491 and 1535 (a further Act of 1594 relating to liferent of a house having been repealed). Significantly, the *cautio* is the only competent remedy of a **fiar** in respect of alleged failures by the liferenter to maintain the subjects in good repair. The fiar cannot, for example, in the course of the liferent, bring an action for specific implement or damages.

Caution. (pr. as in "nation")

Security, in civil matters. Cautionry is the obligation by which one becomes surety for another and is normally in the form of a bond.

Caveat.

A legal document lodged in court by a party so that no order or ruling affecting him passes in his absence or without his receiving prior notice.

Caveat emptor

Let the buyer beware. A rule greatly qualified both at common law and by statute.

Certification.

(i) The assurance given to a party of the course to be followed in case he disobeys the will of the summons or other writ or the order of the court.

(ii) The term for the motion by which additional remuneration is sought for a skilled witness attending at a proof or jury trial.

Certiorate.

To give formal notice of a fact to another.

Cess.

Land tax, now abolished.

Cessio bonorum.

Meaning "a surrender of goods or estate". An obsolete action in which an insolvent debtor brought his creditors into court to surrender his assets to them in order to avoid imprisonment for debt.

Cestui que trust.

A term of English law sometimes used in Scotland to signify the person who possesses the equitable or beneficial right to property held in trust. See **Beneficiary**.

Chamberlain ("The Chamberlain of Scotland").

The name of a former officer-of-state having the duty of inspecting royal burghs, inquiring into the conduct of magistrates and seeing to the due application of the burgh revenues. The title was also sometimes used of the treasurer of a burgh prior to the reorganisation of local government in 1975.

Chancellor.

An obsolete term for the foreman of a jury. There has been no high officer of state with the title of Chancellor in Scotland since 1707.

Chancery.

An office originally directed by the Lord Chancellor of Scotland, but surviving him. Formerly, questions of property were tried on brieves issuing from the chancery and directing an inferior judge to try some issue with a jury. This procedure has for long been obsolete but the chancery continued to deal with the service of heirs and the recording of services. The office of Sheriff of Chancery created in 1847 with duties in regard to service of heirs and Crown charters is now absorbed in the office of the Sheriff of Lothian and Borders. With the abolition since 1964 of the special position of the heir in heritage, petitions for service, although still competent in certain circumstances, are rare but certain Crown writs and commissions continue to be issued from the Chancery Office by the official functioning as Director of Chancery.

Charge.

(i) An order to obey a decree of the court. Prior to its abolition a charge was a pre-requisite of poinding, i.e. a written command in name of the sovereign that required the debtor to pay or perform in a given time.

(ii) In a jury trial the address by the presiding judge to the jury, directing them particularly on matters of law.

(iii) In company law the English use of the term as signifying a debt secured on some property has now been statutorily imported into Scotland in provisions for the registration of charges and the creation of floating charges.

(iv) In criminal law the accusation of crime initiating a prosecution.

Charge and discharge, Account.

See **Account of charge and discharge**.

Charter.

(i) In feudal law, a deed granted by a superior for a variety of purposes, as of an original grant of the land, or a re-grant, or entering a purchaser. See **Charter by progress;** *Novodamus*.

(ii) A grant by the Crown incorporating a group or body of persons as a company.

Charter by progress.

The charter of confirmation and the charter of resignation were called charters by progress because they were used to renew a right to land previously held, as distinguished from an original charter by which a right was created.

Charterparty.

A document evidencing a contract whereby a ship or some principal part thereof is let to a charterer until the expiry of a fixed period or for one or more voyages.

Chartulary.

A mediaeval book or register containing copies of charters and other deeds granted by the owner of landed estate.

Child stealing.

See *Plagium*.

Chirographum apud debitorem repertum presumitur solutum.

Where a written obligation to repay a debt is found in that debtor's possession, the fact gives rise to the presumption that the debt has been repaid and the written obligation returned to the debtor by the creditor.

Circuit court.

A criminal court held by a judge of the High Court of Justiciary outwith Edinburgh. In the past circuit courts would pass through the country periodically, but in modern times due to volume of business they sit more often than not. The High Court of Justiciary has for many years been sitting permanently in Glasgow.

Circumstantial evidence (*facta probationis*).

Evidence of circumstances providing indirect or presumptive evidence of some fact of which direct evidence, (e.g. eyewitness evidence) is lacking. Circumstantial evidence may allow inferences to be drawn in relation to a crucial fact. See **Crucial evidence**.

Circumvention.

See **Facility and circumvention**.

Cite.

(i) To summon to court, whether of party, witness, or juror.

(ii) To refer in argument to some authority such as a statute or decided case.

Civil law.

(i) Private law concerned with the rights and duties of individuals and the settlement of their disputes and distinguishable on the one hand from public law concerning matters involving the state or an agent of the state and on the other hand from criminal law dealing with the recognition and treatment of crimes and offences.

(ii) Roman law generally, but particularly as adapted and studied in the mediaeval period.

(iii) The law of a state, i.e. civilian law, hence including municipal law.

***Clare constat*, Precept of.**

A deed granted by a superior to the heir of a deceased vassal setting forth that it "clearly appears" that the applicant for the precept is lawful heir. Upon this sasine was taken. A writ of *clare constat* was a later statutory elaboration which had the advantage of confirming all deeds necessary to a good title. With the abolition since 1964 of the special position of the heir in heritage the function of these documents ceased to exist and the relevant statutory provisions have been repealed.

Clause.

(i) A part or section of a deed or instrument. The following names of clauses are perhaps not self-explanatory and therefore, worth mentioning: a *clause of devolution* is one "devolving" an office or duty on X upon failure of A to do some act; a *clause of return* is one by which the granter of a right provides that in certain circumstances it shall return or revert to himself; *clauses irritant and resolutive*, found in deeds such as feu charters and leases, render void acts done contrary to the provisions of the deed and take away (*resolve*) the rights of the offender.

(ii) The equivalent in a Bill of a section in an Act.

Cleared date (cleared funds).

The date on which monies required for a given withdrawal are removed from the bank account in which they have been held. Such monies are then referred to as "cleared funds".

Clerk of Justiciary.

The principal clerk of court in the High Court of Justiciary, the office being now combined with that of the principal **Clerk of Session**.

Clerk of Session.

The principal clerk of court in the Court of Session, the office being now combined with that of the principal **Clerk of Justiciary**.

Clerk Register, Lord.

Now an honorary role, this was once an important officer of state, having been at various epochs Keeper of the Great and other Seals, Clerk of Parliament, and custodian of the Registers, to name only these. From 1879 onwards he was shorn of all practical duties except that of presiding over the election of representative Scottish peers and that function disappeared with the Peerage Act of 1963 admitting all Scottish peers to the House of Lords. In 1928, out of the office of Lord Clerk Register, came the office of Keeper of the Registers and Records of Scotland. This office in turn was divided in 1948 into the offices of **Keeper of the Registers of Scotland** and **Keeper of the Records of Scotland**.

Clerk to the Signet.

See **Signet**.

Close season.

The period of the year defined in statutes dealing with various kinds of fish and game during which it is unlawful to take or kill the kind of fish or game in question.

Codicil.

A document altering, adding to or revoking an existing testamentary document. See **Testament**.

Codifying Act.

An Act that puts all the law from statutory or other sources, possibly amended, into one Act. See **Consolidation Act**.

Cognate.

A relative through the mother. See **Agnate**.

Cognition.

A judicial process now obsolete by which a man might be found insane by a jury and a curator might be appointed.

Cognitionis causa tantum.

Applies to an action of declarator raised for the purpose of constituting a debt or claim against the estate of a deceased person.

Collateral.

(i) In regard to succession a person of the same ancestry but not of the same direct line of descent as the deceased person, e.g. his brothers, sisters or cousins and their children. It is sometimes used to include descendants of collaterals and brothers and sisters of ascendants.

(ii) In regard to securities; a *collateral security* is an additional and separate security for the due performance of an obligation.

Collatio (or **collation**) ***inter haeredes.***

The bringing of heritage into one common stock with the moveables so that the heir in heritage might share in the moveable succession with the heirs in moveables. Collation of this kind became unnecessary with the assimilation of heritage and moveables as regards succession resulting from the provisions of the Succession (Scotland) Act 1964.

Collatio (or **collation**) ***inter liberos.***

Relates to the sum available for ***legitim***—the legitim fund—and is the crediting to that fund of any provision received in advance, during the parent's or grandparent's life, by one who later claims on the fund.

College of Justice.

A formal name of the Court of Session. The College of Justice includes advocates, writers to the signet, clerks, and others, as well as the judges.

Commissary.

Originally an ecclesiastical judge having jurisdiction in such matters as legitimacy, succession and declarators of marriage. His place has been taken partly by the sheriff, partly by the Court of Session. The commissary offices are departments of the sheriff clerk's offices that deal with inventories of the estates of deceased persons and issue confirmation of appointment of executors.

Commission for taking proof.

A warrant or authorisation by the court of some qualified person to take the evidence of witnesses. It is always coupled with a diligence that enables witnesses to be cited and documents to be called for.

Commissioner, Lord High.

The representative of the Sovereign in the **General Assembly of the Church of Scotland**.

Commissioners in a sequestration.

Persons, not more than five in number, who may be appointed by the creditors in a sequestration pursuant to the Bankruptcy (Scotland) Act 1985 to advise the permanent trustee.

Commit.

To order a man's consignment to prison either to await further inquiry into the case (committal for further examination) or until he is liberated in due course of law (full committal).

Commixtion.

Mixture of property belonging to different people with results upon property rights that vary with circumstances.

Commodate (or *Commodatum*).

A loan made gratuitously of an article which must be returned exactly as lent.

Common agent.

A solicitor appointed in processes where there are several claimants with common interests as in ranking and sale, locality of stipend and **multiplepoinding**. He acts for those having common interests.

Common calamity.

An incident in which two or more related persons die apparently simultaneously giving rise to certain problems of succession for which statute seeks to provide. If they were husband and wife, neither is presumed to have survived the other; otherwise, generally the younger is presumed to have died after the older.

Common debtor.

Where property of a debtor has been arrested by one creditor in the hands of a third party and there are several other creditors also claiming a share, the debtor is referred to as the "common debtor".

Common good.

Property formerly of a **burgh**, now of a district or island council, derived from some source other than the rates.

Common interest.

An interest, as of adjoining users of a common wall or floor, not amounting to property, but entitling the party interested to a say in the use of the thing.

Common law.

The rules of law not derived from statute but from other sources such as judicial decisions, authoritative writings, Roman law or custom.

Common property.

Common ownership in a thing or land, without demarcation of shares and characterised especially by the existence of a right in any common owner to compel a division of the common property. See *Pro indiviso*; **Joint property**.

Commonty.

Virtually obsolete, a right (neither common property nor common interest) of joint perpetual use conferred by the proprietor of land for the common use of many.

Communicate.

To make some right available to another in fulfilment of a legal duty or to pass on or hand over as of some advantage.

Communings.

An expression sometimes applied to negotiations leading up to a contract.

Community law.

The rules of law existing under the treaties establishing the European Communities (now the European Union). See **European Court of Justice**.

Commute.

To convert into some other form, e.g. the commutation of feudal casualties when the casualty was replaced by an addition to the annual feuduty or extinguished by a single payment.

Compear.

Of a defender, to appear in the action.

Compensatio injuriarum.

A now obsolete plea of set-off, on account of mutual injuries based on the proposition that a defender should not be compelled to pay damages to a pursuer who is liable in as great or greater damages to the defender. A defender can now rely on statutory contributory negligence. See **Contributory**.

Compensation.

The extinction of mutual similar claims by setting of one against the other where there is *concursus debiti et crediti*. See **Set-off**.

Competent and omitted.

A form of procedural bar in civil matters, where the pursuer is prevented from putting forward a ground of action that could have been pled (but was not) in an earlier case between the same parties. Such pleas in the new action are thus barred as "competent and omitted".

Complaint.

A document instituting summary criminal proceedings in a sheriff or district court setting out the offence charged and signed by the Procurator fiscal. See **Indictment**.

Composition.

(i) A casualty formerly payable to a superior by a buyer of land on entering upon the estate as a vassal.

(ii) A proportion of his debts that an insolvent offers to his creditors and which, if accepted and approved by the court, forms the basis of a settlement without sequestration running its course.

Concert.

See **Art and part**.

Conclusion.

The conclusion in a Court of Session summons is the statement of the precise relief sought. *To conclude for* is to claim in this fashion. See **Crave**.

Concourse.

Has two meanings:

(i) the simultaneous existence of two actions based on the same grounds; and

(ii) the concurrence of the public prosecutor in a private prosecution.

Concursus debiti et crediti.

In a question of compensation it is necessary that the parties be at the same time, debtor and creditor, one of the other, and debtor and creditor in the same capacity. This is the concourse of debit and credit. See **Set-off**.

Condescendence.

The part of a pursuer's written pleadings that contains a statement of the facts on which he relies.

Condictio.

An action or claim directed against a person, e.g. for payment of a sum of money as contrasted with a real action sometimes called **vindicatio**. For example, the *condictio indebiti*, a term of civil law meaning an action for repayment of money paid in error.

Conditio si institutus.

See *Si sine liberis decesserit*.

Conditio si testator.

See *Si sine liberis decesserit*.

Conditional institute.

See **Institute**.

Confident.

See **Conjunct and confident**.

Confirmation.

The process whereby executors are judicially recognised or confirmed in their office and receive a title to the property and assets of the deceased person.

Conform.

In conformity. Commonly in the expression *decree conform*, a judgment by one court given to render effective the judgment of another.

Confusio.

(i) Commixtion of liquids.

(ii) A mode of extinguishing a debt, right or claim where either party acquires the title of the other by inheritance or otherwise.

Conjoin.

To order that two processes involving the same subject-matter and the same parties be tried together.

Conjunct.

Joint. Thus, *conjunct fee* and **liferent** exists where there is a joint fee in two or more during their lives, the survivor taking a fee of one half with a liferent of the other.

Conjunct and confident.

Of a person, to be related by blood and connected by interest to another.

Conjunct and several.

See **Joint and several obligation**.

Conjunct probation or proof.

The process of disproving by evidence an opponent's averments, carried on as part of the process of proving a party's own case. Also see **Replication, proof in**.

Consanguinean.

A brother or sister is consanguinean with another where they have a common father but different mothers. See **Uterine**.

Consensus in idem.

The state of agreement on essentials as between contracting parties necessary for the validity and enforceability of the contract.

Consignation.

(i) The deposit in court or with a third party under court authority of money (or an article) in dispute.

(ii) The deposit in a bank in joint names of purchaser and seller of the price of a heritable property where completion of a sale transaction is for some reason delayed.

Consistorial.

Is derived from *consistorium*, the place where the Emperor's council met. The bishops used it for their courts and thence the adjective consistorial came to be used as descriptive of the court of the commissaries and of the actions that were tried there. In modern use, as applied to actions, it has been narrowed down to mean actions between husband and wife that involve status.

Consolidation.

(i) The vesting in one person of a superiority, or *dominum directum*, of land together with the *dominum utile* or beneficial ownership.

(ii) A Consolidation Act is one that repeals and re-enacts in one statute the provisions of a number of statutes on the same subject. See **Codifying Act**.

Constitute.

To determine or establish a debt, usually by means of the judgment of a court. Especially of the case where the action is to be directed against the successors of a deceased debtor.

Constructive.

Effective in law although not existing in fact.

Consultation.

(i) The power that the judges of a Division of the Inner House of the Court of Session have to invoke the opinion of or consult other judges in a case where there is especial difficulty or where the judges of the Division are equally divided.

(ii) A meeting between counsel and solicitor with or without the client to discuss a case.

Consumer.

Those who buy, obtain and use all kinds of goods and services. The area of law comprising elements of contract, delict and criminal law developed to safeguard their interests, is sometimes described as consumer protection law (including also the regulation of consumer credit transactions of all kinds).

Contact.

See **Access**.

Contemporanea expositio.

Embodies the rule that statutes, deeds or contracts should in case of doubt be given the meaning that they had or were given at the time when they were made.

Contempt of court.

(i) Conduct that challenges or affronts the authority of the court (any court) or the supremacy of the law itself, every court having an inherent power to punish persons who are in contempt of it.

(ii) In the criminal sense, words or acts obstructing or tending to obstruct the administration of justice, e.g. by prejudicing an accused person's prospects of a fair trial.

(iii) In civil proceedings, disregard of an order of court or breach of an undertaking given to the court. See **Contumacy**.

Contestatio (**Contestation**).

See **Litiscontestation**.

Contingency.

(i) A similarity in the subject-matter of actions that may lead the court to remit the later in time, *ob contingentiam*, to the court dealing with the earlier. Alternatively, where actions are contingent, the court may sist one action to await the outcome in the other.

(ii) An uncertain event on which the existence of some right depends.

Continue.

To postpone decision in judicial proceedings and adjourn them to a later date for further action.

Contra bonos mores.

The principle on which contracts or obligations given for an immoral consideration are unenforceable, being contrary to morality. See ***Turpis causa***.

Contra proferentem.

The rule whereby an indefinite or doubtful provision in a document should be construed against the party responsible for its inclusion.

Contract.

An agreement based on consent between two or more individuals or entities (having legal capacity), in which an offer is made and accepted. A contract need not be written; it can be oral or implied from the actings of the parties to it. Some contracts, however, require to be in writing and formally executed in order to have validity, e.g. a contract for the sale of heritable property. The law of contract forms part of the wider law of obligations, which encompasses obligations arising from consent (such as contract) and obligations that are implied by law (such as delict, quasi-contract and quasi-delict). See **Delict; Unjustified enrichment; Quasi-contract; Quasi-delict**.

Contributory.

(i) In company law a person liable as member or shareholder to contribute to the company's assests in its winding up.

(ii) In delict contributory negligence on the part of the claimant, formerly a bar to the claim, is now a ground for reduction of the damages to be awarded. See *Compensatio injuriarum*.

Contumacy.

A person is guilty of contumacy, or *contumacious*, when he refuses obedience to a legal citation.

Conventional.

Of obligations, arising out of agreement or contract as opposed to those imposed by law, such as those in delict or unjustified enrichment. See **Obediential**.

Corporeal.

The adjective applicable to heritable and moveable property which are also physical objects. See **Incorporeal**.

Corroboration.

(i) In court proceedings evidence, whether verbal, documentary or real, confirmatory of other evidence given. The corroborating evidence must come from a separate source. For example, one confession by an accused to one person cannot be corroborated by the same confession by the accused to another person. Both confessions, though spoken to by different witnesses, are from the same source, i.e. the accused.

(ii) In conveyancing practice the Bond of Corroboration creates a new or additional personal obligation in respect of an existing Bond, the existence of which it confirms.

Council of Europe.

The Council of Europe should not be confused with the European Union. The Council is an inter-governmental organisation presently comprised of 45 member states (including the 15 member states of the

European Union) responsible for drawing up conventions to which the member states may accede, notably in the fields of human rights, culture and democracy. See **European Convention on Human Rights**.

Council of the European Union.

One of the five Institutions of the European Union, the Council is the main decision making body. It is comprised of single representatives of the member states of the European Union who act as delegates of the governments of those states. Which minister attends which meeting depends upon the subject on the agenda. For example, if the Council is to discuss environmental issues, the meeting will be attended by the environment minister for each state.

Counsel.

In Scotland a member of the Faculty of Advocates practising at the Bar.

Count reckoning and payment, Action of.

An action brought to compel the defender to give an account of his dealing with property under his control, and pay any balance found due.

Courtesy.

The **liferent** enjoyed by a widower of the heritage of his late wife, abolished with the assimilation of heritable and moveable succession by the Succession (Scotland) Act 1964.

Crave.

To ask formally of a court; in Sheriff Court practice the part of the initial writ corresponding to the conclusion in a Court of Session summons is called the crave.

Creditor.

A person to whom another person as debtor is obliged in some monetary or other obligation.

Crimen falsi.

A general term covering any offence involving falsehood, e.g. forgery, perjury, falsehood, fraud and wilful imposition, etc.

Croft.

A special form of agricultural holding governed by the Crofters Acts and located within the seven counties in Scotland designated as crofting counties (Argyll, Caithness, Inverness, Orkney, Ross and Cromarty, Shetland and Sutherland), the tenant or crofter or his predecessors having provided the buildings and fixed equipment. A crofter, among others, has the right to purchase the croft of which he is tenant and thus become owner. See **Agricultural holding**.

Crown.

(i) The Sovereign.

(ii) Of the United Kingdom state generally; in relation to rights, interests, privileges, criminal proceedings, etc. means the state as represented by Her Majesty's government and known as "the Crown in right of Her Majesty's Government" in the United Kingdom.

(iii) As regards the devolved Scottish government, the **Scottish Administration**, referred to as "the Crown in right of the Scottish Administration".

Crown Agent Designate.

The chief Crown solicitor in criminal matters and head of legal staff at Crown Office.

Crown Counsel.

See **Advocate Depute**.

Crucial evidence.

Also referred to as "the facts in issue" (*facta probanda*) "essential facts" or "crucial facts". In criminal proceedings, the crucial evidence or the crucial facts are those facts that are required to be proved in order to establish that a crime has been committed. The crucial facts are essentially two:

(i) has a crime been committed; and

(ii) who committed it.

The crucial facts require to be corroborated. In civil proceedings the crucial facts are the facts that a party must or ought to aver in order to make a case relevant to go to proof. See **Circumstantial evidence**.

Culpa.

Fault or negligence, being the absence of care or diligence not to cause or permit harm to persons or not to breach the common law duty to take reasonable care in particular circumstances. The law has historically recognised three levels of culpability drawn from Roman law:

(i) *culpa lata*, which is gross fault or negligence equal to **Dole**;

(ii) *culpa levis*, which is the degree of negligence that a person may be guilty of, even when ordinarily attending to his own affairs; and

(iii) *culpa levissima*, the slightest degree of fault or negligence that may be fallen into by one who manages his affairs with the greatest attention and prudence. See **Delict; Negligence; Quasi-delict**.

Culpable homicide.

The killing of a human being, neither casual or justifiable but falling short of the malicious evil intention required to constitute murder. It is similar to the English crime of manslaughter.

Curator.

A person either entitled by law or appointed by the court or an individual to administer the estate of another, as of a young or insane person.

Curator ad litem.

A person appointed by the court to look after the interests of a party to proceedings who is under legal disability but has no guardian.

Curator bonis.

The person appointed by the court to manage the estate of a young person in place of his legal guardian or to manage the estate of a person above minority suffering from mental or, less commonly, bodily infirmity. Following the introduction of the Adults with Incapacity (Scotland) Act 2000 it is no longer competent to create *curators bonis.*

Custody.

(i) In criminal law the detention, by the police, of a person suspected or accused of a crime or offence.

(ii) In family law the right of one or other of separated parents to have a child of their marriage living with him or her in family.

Cy près. (pr. "see-pray")

A doctrine of the law of trusts, evolved in English law but also adopted in Scotland, whereby if a gift or bequest is clearly for a purely public purpose (including a charitable purpose) it will not be allowed to fail because the precise object to be benefited or the mode of application of the funds is uncertain or impracticable. Application is to the *nobile officium* of the Court of Session for variation of the trust to a purpose or application as close as possible to the apparent intention of the truster.

D

Damages.

Money claimed as compensation for loss, injury or damage resulting from breach of duty, legal or contractual.

Damnum.

Harm, loss or injury.

Damnum absque injuria.

Loss or damage without legal wrong (i.e. the element of *injuria*) for which no claim can be made.

Damnum fatale.

A loss due to an unusual accident such as the occurrence of exceptional storm or flood, sometimes referred to by the English law term "**Act of God**".

Damnum injuria datum.

The founding principle of the law of reparation for delicts. Reparation is that which makes good, so far as possible in terms of money, loss (*damnum*) caused (*datum*) by a legal wrong (*injuria*). All three elements are essential before liability to make reparation arises. See *Damnum*; *Injuria.*

Dead's part of gear.

The part of his moveables that a man has power to leave by will, being:
(i) one-third if he leaves both wife and children;

(ii) one-half if he leaves wife or children only; and

(iii) the whole if he leaves neither wife nor children.

Dean of Faculty.

The leader of the Scottish Bar, as elected by the members of the Faculty of Advocates.

Dean of Guild.

A judge in certain burghs, formerly possessed of an important jurisdiction in mercantile disputes, and until the reorganisation of local government possessed of an important jurisdiction in the matter of building safety.

Debitum fundi (or *Debitum reale*).

A real debt or obligation secured over land that attaches to the land itself, as for example, a feuduty.

Debt.

Money legally owed by one person (the debtor) to another (the creditor). See **Document of debt**.

Decern.

Of a court, to decree; an extremely formal verb meaning to give final decree or judgment, formerly but no longer necessary to warrant the issue of an extract of decree or judgement.

Declaration.

The statement made in presence of the sheriff, at or after his first appearance in court, by a person whom it is intended to try on indictment.

Declarator, Action of.

An action brought by an interested party to have some legal right declared but without claim on any person called as defender to do anything. There requires to be a practical purpose in seeking declarator. The declarator of the court does not of itself enforce the right.

Declinature.

(i) The refusal by a judge to exercise jurisdiction, appropriate in a case in which by reason of relationship to a party or pecuniary or other possible interest his decision might be thought to be affected.

(ii) Refusal to accept some office, appointment or benefit, e.g. as a trustee nominated by the truster.

Decree.

The common Scottish technical term for a final judgment. (The word as a term of art is accented on the first syllable.) Thus *decree arbitral*, the decision of an arbiter; *decree conform*, a decree given by the Court of Session in aid of a lower court to enable diligence to be done; *decree dative*, the judgment appointing a person executor. For Decree of Dismissal, see **Absolvitor**.

De die in diem.
Literally "from day to day"; a basis on which payments such as interest on money is calculated.

Deed.
A formal document, executed and authenticated in accordance with prescribed formalities and incorporating the terms of an agreement, contract or obligation.

Deed of arrangement.
A contract between competing claimants or parties in dispute whereby issues such as the distribution of funds or property are agreed.

Deeming.
A common form of legal fiction whereby, e.g. in terms of a statute one thing may be deemed to be another.

De facto.
In point of fact; actual. See **De jure**.

Defamation.
The publication or communication of a false statement or idea which is injurious to the party to whom it refers or relates. Defamation can either be in the form of libel (written defamation) or slander (spoken defamation). Unlike in England, no distinction is made in Scots law between the two forms.

Defences.
The statement by way of defence lodged by the defender being the party against whom a civil action is brought. The plural signifies, presumably, that the defender may rely on more legal answers than one.

De fideli.
Short for *de fideli administratione officii;* the oath *de fideli administratione* is an oath taken by persons appointed to perform certain public or other duties that they will faithfully carry them out, e.g. shorthand writers in court, curators appointed by the court.

Deforcement.
A crime consisting of resistance to officers of the law whilst executing their duty in civil matters.

De jure.
In point of law: legal as opposed to actual. See **De facto**.

Del credere.
An arrangement under which an agent guarantees to his principal the performance of a third party when he contracts on the principal's behalf.

Delectus personae.
Choice of a particular person for reasons specific to that individual. Important in a legal sense as preventing assignation or delegation of a duty by the person chosen.

Delegation.

(i) A form of novation that consists in the extinction of the liability of one party to a contract by the substitution of the liability of another.

(ii) Where an agent competently delegates authority to a sub-agent, creating a contract between that sub-agent and the principal. This is in exception to the general common law rule *delegatus non potest delegare* (a person to whom a matter has been delegated cannot himself delegate it).

Delict.

Arising from the law of obligations, A delict is a civil wrong caused by the deliberate or negligent breach of a duty imposed by law, either through action or omission. The wrongdoer incurs the obligation to make reparation to the injured party. See *Damnum injuria datum*. The term was formerly used to refer to criminal wrongs generally. The English term is **Tort**. See *Culpa*; **Negligence**.

Deliverance.

A decision of or order by a court. See **Decree; Interlocutor**.

Delivery.

(i) The act affecting transfer of possession of a corporeal moveable thing from one person to another.

(ii) The normal requisite for the effectiveness of a deed, being the acknowledgement of a person by words or conduct of his intention to be bound by a deed or recording of the deed itself in the appropriate register.

De minimis.

An abbreviation of the brocard *de minimis non curat lex*, "the law ignores trifles".

De novo.

Of new, afresh.

Denude.

Of a trustee, to hand over the trust estate on giving up the office of trustee.

De plano.

Immediately, summarily or without further procedure.

Deponent.

A party such as a witness making a deposition.

Deposit or Depositation.

(i) A gratuitous contract under which a corporeal moveable is entrusted by one (the depositor) to another (the depository or depositary).

(ii) Money given as a pledge.

(iii) The first payment in a hire purchase agreement.

(iv) A payment to the credit of a bank account.

Deposition.

A statement usually by a witness, made on oath and recorded in writing, e.g. where a witness is dying and his evidence must be obtained for the purpose of a later trial.

De presenti.

At present, now.

De recenti.

Recent. Sometimes applied to a statement of a witness or party involved made shortly after an occurrence and so having enhanced credibility.

Dereliction.

Abandonment of something owned.

Desert.

To *desert the diet* (the only particular use of this verb) is to give up a criminal charge, either ***pro loco et tempore***, when a fresh charge can be brought or simpliciter, which is final and prevents the charge being brought again.

Design.

To set forth a person's full name, occupation and address in writing in order to clearly identify him. Whence designation. The designation of a witness need only comprise his name and address.

Destination.

A direction as to the persons who are to succeed to moveable and/or heritable property; usually found in a will, disposition or other deed affecting heritable property.

Destination over.

A destination to one person on failure of a precedent gift, usually by will, to another. For example, "to A, whom failing, to B".

Detention.

(i) The punishment of young offenders detained in custody for a period prescribed by the court.

(ii) The lawful intervention of an outside party or agent to ensure that a person stays in a particular place, e.g. detention in a mental institution, or detention by the police for the purpose of questioning.

Devolution.

See **Clause**.

Devolve.

Arbiters are said to devolve their decision to an oversman.

Devolved matters.

Under the devolution settlement, the areas of legislative and governmental competence in which the **Scottish Parliament** and Executive are competent to act. While devolved matters are not expressly defined, the areas of legislative and governmental competence reserved by Westminster and the UK government are. See **Reserved matters**.

Dies cedit; Dies venit.
Dies cedit means that a right has vested in a person: *dies venit* means that it has become enforceable.

Dies non.
A non legal day, e.g. a Sunday or a public holiday.

Diet.
The date for hearing of a case for any one of a variety of purposes, fixed by the court.

Dilatory.
Used of defences in a civil action, meaning purely technical, not touching the merits and designed to delay proceedings. See **Peremptory**.

Diligence.
Execution against debtors; also a process for procuring the recovery of writings from an opponent or third party or for obtaining the evidence of witnesses before a commissioner. See **Arrestment; Adjudication; Inhibition; Attachment**.

Diminished responsibility.
Mental weakness short of insanity which may justify the offence of murder being reduced to that of **culpable homicide** or otherwise mitigate criminal guilt.

Direct effect.
The quality of EU law which confers upon the citizen a right or rights that national courts must protect. *Vertical direct effect* describes where a right lies against a member state; and *horizontal direct effect* where a right lies against another citizen or other natural or legal person.

Discharge.
(i) The termination of liability under contract by receipt for payment or other document.
(ii) The release of a person from debt or obligation or from imprisonment or from the disabilities of bankruptcy.

Discuss.
To proceed against one of two possible debtors, such as a principal debtor and a cautioner, as a preliminary to going against the other. See **Caution**.

Dispone.
Of land, to convey, transferring the right of ownership from the disponer to the disponee. Formerly an essential word in any valid conveyance of land.

Disposition.
A unilateral deed by which property, heritable or moveable, is alienated.

Dispositive clause.
The operative clause of a deed by which property is conveyed.

District.
A subdivision of region for purposes of local government, the authority being the district council.

District court.
The court in each district or island area dealing with minor criminal offences and replacing the burgh or magistrates courts as existing before the local government reorganisation of 1975. District courts are presided over by Justices of the Peace, except in Glasgow where Stipendiary Magistrates are appointed. See **Justices of the Peace; Stipendiary magistrate**.

Division, Action of.
An action by which common property is divided.

Docquet (or Docket).
(i) An addition to or endorsement on a deed or other document, e.g. on a will vicariously subscribed for someone unable to write or on a confirmation of executors transferring heritable property to a beneficiary.
(ii) Occasionally used to describe an abstract or summary of a longer document.

Document of debt.
A document which constitutes evidence of a legal transaction or by which the indebtedness is created, e.g. a bill of exchange. Loosely used.

Dole.
Evil intention, *malus animus*, malice in the legal sense. The nearest Scottish equivalent to the English concept of **mens rea**, e.g. the intention or state of mind required to constitute a particular crime.

Domicile.
The territorial jurisdiction of a legal system (e.g. Scotland) in which a person is regarded as having his permanent home, with that legal system consequently regulating many questions affecting him personally.

Dominant tenement.
A piece of land with the ownership of which goes a servitude right over adjoining land, the servient tenement. See **Servitude**.

Dominium directum.
In feudal law, the right of land enjoyed by the superior.

Dominium utile.
The substantial right in land enjoyed by the vassal which would be known popularly as ownership.

Dominus litis.
The person really, though not nominally, responsible for instituting or carrying on legal proceedings, liable to be ordered to pay expenses;

effectively the person who derives the benefit of a favourable judgement and is liable for the effects of an adverse judgement.

Donation inter vivos.

A gift made by one living person to another.

Donation *mortis causa*.

A gift made conditionally on the donee surviving the donor.

Donatory.

A person to whom property falling to the Crown, as by forfeiture or failure of succession, is given by the Crown.

Doom.

The judgment or sentence of a court both as regards civil and criminal causes. *Falsing of dooms* was formerly used to signify the taking of an appeal to a higher tribunal.

Double.

A copy.

Double distress.

Two or more competing claims on a single fund, an essential of a **multiplepoinding**.

Drove road.

A road or passageway over private property originally intended for the passage of farmers' stock to or from markets and constituting a public right of way or a servitude according as it is available to farmers in the district generally or only to the occupiers of certain properties.

Duress.

See **Force or Fear**.

Dying declaration.

The statement of a witness made on his deathbed which may be admissible in subsequent criminal proceedings: if made on oath and subscribed it will be termed a dying deposition.

E

Eavesdrop.

See **Stillicide**.

Edictal citation.

A mode of citing in the Scottish courts persons who are abroad or whose whereabouts are unknown but who are subject to the courts' jurisdiction. It is done by sending copies of the summons to the office of the Keeper of Edictal Citations, who is the Extractor of the Court of Session.

Effeiring to. (pr. "eff-airing")

Relating or appertaining to.

Effeirs, As.

Literally, as relates or corresponds; duly, in the proper way, in due form.

Eik. (pr. "eek")

An extension of the confirmation of an executor to cover property not originally included.

Ejection.

(i) Unlawful and violent casting out of a possessor from his heritage: leading to an action of ejection for its recovery. This action arises out of an ejection: it is not an action brought to secure ejection.

(ii) The executive warrant following upon a decree in an action of removing against a tenant on the termination of his lease or when an irritancy is incurred.

(iii) An action to remove persons occupying land or buildings without title. See **Removing**.

Ejusdem generis.

Of the same kind. The rule of interpretation whereby general words following an enumeration of particulars are read as limited to the same general category as the particulars.

Election.

See **Approbate** and **Reprobate**.

Elide.

To oust or exclude.

Embezzle.

To fraudulently turn to one's own use money or property lawfully handed over for another purpose.

Encumbrance.

A burden, usually a debt, secured over land and thus encumbering it.

Engross.

To write or type a deed or a document complete in its final form and ready for signature or execution.

Enorm.

See **Lesion**.

Entail.

See *Tailzie*.

Entitled spouse.

The spouse entitled by virtue of ownership, tenancy or other authority to occupy a matrimonial home. See **Non-entitled spouse**.

Entry.
(i) In feudal law, the establishment of an heir or singular successor according to the rules of land tenure, as a new vassal with his superior; since 1874 this has been implied from infeftment.
(ii) The taking of possession of land as of right by a party such as a purchaser or lessee.

Equipollent.
A legal synonym for equivalent.

Escheat. (pr. "is-cheat")
Forfeiture or confiscation.

Estate.
A person's whole assets including both heritable and moveable property.

Esto.
Used in written pleadings to signify "if it be so".

European Commission.
One of the five Institutions of the European Union, it is a politically independent body that represents and upholds the interests of the European Union as a whole. The Commission proposes legislation, policies and programmes of action and is responsible for implementing the decisions of the **European Parliament** and **Council of the European Union**.

European Convention on Human Rights.
The Convention for the Protection of Human Rights and Fundamental Freedoms, signed in Rome in 1950, to which all the member states of the **Council of Europe** are party. Whilst the European Union is not party to the Convention, the rights enumerated in it are deemed to form a part of EU law. The Convention became part of the domestic law of Scotland as a result of the devolution settlement in 1998 inasmuch as it binds members of the **Scottish Executive** to comply therewith in their actions (s.57(2) of the Scotland Act 1998). The Convention was adopted into UK law by the Human Rights Act 1998.

European Court of Auditors.
One of the five Institutions of the European Union, it audits the European Union's revenue and expenditure in order to monitor its lawful and regular management. The Court was established in 1977.

European Court of Human Rights.
A court created by the **Council of Europe** comprising judges with jurisdiction over the interpretation and application of the **European Convention on Human Rights**.

European Court of Justice.
One of the five Institutions of the European Union (together with the **European Parliament, European Commission, Council of the European Union** and **European Court of Auditors**), it is entrusted

with ensuring that, in the interpretation and application of its treaties, the law of the European Union is interpreted and applied in the same way in each member state. The Court has power to settle disputes involving member states, EU institutions, businesses and individuals. It is composed of one judge per member state in order that all EU national legal systems are represented. The Court is assisted by "*Advocates General*". Their role is to present public and impartial reasoned opinions on the case before the Court.

European Parliament.
One of the five institutions of the European Union. Formerly known as the "Assembly", it consists of elected members from the citizens of the European Union's member states. It holds monthly plenary sessions in Strasbourg, committee and additional plenary sessions in Brussels and has its General Secretariat in Luxembourg. There are presently 626 members, with that figure set to increase to 786 by 2009.

Evidents.
Writs and title-deeds, evidence of heritable rights. Practically obsolete.

Ex adverso.
Signifies "opposite to" with reference to land or buildings.

Ex aebudante cautela.
Superfluous or unnecessary caution.

Examination.
The interrogation in court of a person called as a witness, which may comprise examination in chief on behalf of the person calling the witness, cross-examination by the opponent or opponents of that party and re-examination on behalf of the first party.

Excambion.
The contract under which one piece of land is exchanged for another.

Exception.
(i) A form of defence to an action. *Ope exceptionis*, by way of exception, being the expression sometimes used. In effect it is a partial admission, e.g. the defender admits the existence of a written agreement to pay money to the pursuer, but states that he has already paid the money to the pursuer.
(ii) A mode of procedure by which legal objection to the verdict of a jury is brought under review by the **Inner House** of the Court of Session, formerly by Bill and now by Note of Exception(s).

Exchequer, Court of.
A court, now merged in the Court of Session, which was created after the Union of 1707 upon the model of the English Court of Exchequer and charged particularly with the decision of Revenue questions. In the Court of Session such matters are still distinguished as Exchequer Causes and the core of Exchequer causes consists in actions for the recovery of central government taxes due to the Board of Inland

Revenue and the customs, excise and other duties due to the Board of Customs and Excise.

Execution.

(i) The carrying out by an officer of the law of a citation or the like; also the writing in which his fulfilment of the duty is narrated.

(ii) Carrying out of a criminal sentence, a civil judgment being more usually styled diligence.

(iii) The authentication of a deed by signing in accordance with required formalities.

Executor.

A person appointed to administer the property or as it is called the executry of a deceased person, formerly restricted to moveable property but now embracing the whole estate. An executor appointed by testamentary writing of the deceased is termed an *executor nominate* and one appointed by the appropriate court an *executor dative*. An *executor creditor* is a person who by way of diligence for recovery of a debt has himself confirmed as executor usually only to some particular item or part of the deceased's assets.

Ex facie.

Apparently or on the face of some document or writing.

Ex gratia.

A payment made or action taken gratuitously and not in compliance with any legal obligation.

Exhibition.

An action to compel the production of documents.

Ex officio.

As holder of a particular office or appointment.

Exoner.

To discharge of liability. Thus a judicial factor may seek exoneration and discharge at the hands of the court.

Ex parte.

Proceedings are ex parte when the party against whom they are brought is not heard, e.g. in interdict proceedings an interim interdict may be granted ex parte.

Expede.

To draw up, make out, complete, as of some instrument or document.

Expenses.

The Scottish technical expression for the costs of an action, including legal fees, outlays, etc.

Expose.

Put up for sale by auction.

Ex post facto.
Retrospective or affecting something already done.

Ex proprio motu.
By the court's or judge's own initiative, without the need for a request from any party to a cause.

Extortion.
(i) The crime of obtaining by threats money or benefits not legally due.
(ii) Punitive terms in a contract which if relating to interest on money may justify its reduction.

Extract.
A written instrument signed by the proper officer, containing a statement of a decree or other judicial or legal document and if necessary, a warrant to charge the debtor and to execute all competent **diligence** against person or property. To extract is to procure this instrument.

Extra commercium.
Applies to subjects excluded from commercial transactions, examples being public roads and titles of honour.

Extra-judicial.
Not transacted under judicial cognisance or superintendence. The word today occurs perhaps most often in the expression extra-judicial expenses, meaning expenses incurred outwith the normal course of judicial proceedings and as such not normally recoverable by a successful party from his opponent. Also, for example, an extra-judicial settlement, i.e. out of court.

Extrinsic.
(i) When on a reference to his oath a party makes an admission but subject to an explanation, the explanation is *extrinsic* or *intrinsic*, according as it is considered separable or inseparable from what is sworn: extrinsic qualifies the oath, intrinsic does not.
(ii) The term is applied to evidence in aid of the interpretation of a statute or document taken from a source outwith the statute or document as opposed to intrinsically found.

Ex turpi causa non oritur action.
The rule that no right of action arises from an immoral or unlawful act.

F

Facility and circumvention.
In civil law, when one person by a dishonest course of conduct plays upon a facile person in order to secure an advantage there is said to be *facility and circumvention* rendering voidable the contract, will or gift thus induced. Three things must be proved in order to found the plea:

facility (mental weakness), **lesion** (harm or loss) and **circumvention** (deceit or dishonesty).

Fact.

In proceedings of any kind a matter of fact, unless admitted, will be determined on evidence whereas a matter of law will be determined on authority such as statutes or decided cases.

Factor.

(i) One who with possession of goods buys or sells on commission for a principal.

(ii) In Scotland the term is more often applied to a manager acting on behalf of an owner of heritable property. See also **Judicial factor**.

Factoring.

The commercial practice whereby a factor accepts responsibility for debt collecting and related matters on behalf of a customer or principal such as a trader or supplier of goods.

Factory (or **Factory and commission**).

A deed granted by A empowering B to act for him in one or several transactions. The English equivalent **Power of attorney**, seems to be displacing the Scots term.

Factum praestandum.

See *Ad factum praestandum*.

Faculty.

(i) A power that may be exercised at any time.

(ii) A society of lawyers, e.g. the Faculty of Advocates. See **Dean of Faculty**.

Falsa demonstratio.

An error such as an incorrect name or description not prejudicing the effectiveness of a writing or document provided the person or subject matter in question is clearly identifiable.

Fair comment.

A defence to a claim for damages for defamation based on a comment made on certain facts. The defence of fair comment requires proof of three things:

(i) the facts stated are true;

(ii) the comment on or criticism of those facts was honestly made; and

(iii) the comment or criticism related to a matter of public interest.

Falsehood, fraud and wilful imposition.

The technical term for the crime that consists, substantially, in obtaining something (usually money) by false pretences. Of this crime forgery, i.e. putting a false name to a writing, is the most important branch.

Fatal accident inquiry.

An inquiry conducted by a sheriff and initiated by the **Procurator fiscal** into any death that was sudden, suspicious or unexplained, or that occurred in circumstances giving rise to public concern.

Fee.

(i) The full right of property in heritage, as contradistinguished from **liferent**.

(ii) Remuneration for professional services such as those of a solicitor or advocate.

Fee fund.

The account or fund used to finance in part the administration of the Court of Session and arising from the court dues, i.e. sums of money required to be paid by litigants at various stages in proceedings.

Ferae natura.

Describes wild or untamed animals as contrasted with domestic animals kept as pets or workers (*domitae naturae*).

Feu.

In feudal law, a feudal holding. To feu is, strictly, to give out land upon a feudal arrangement whereby the "vassal" (buyer) holds land of his "feudal superior" (the landowner) usually upon the terms that he builds on the land and pays a perpetual rent, or feuduty. He is virtually owner so long as he pays and observes any conditions. A piece of land thus feued is sometimes referred to as a feu. It has, since 1974, been incompetent for a feudal grant to be subject to the imposition of a feuduty and provisions that have been made for their redemption will result eventually in the disappearance of feuduties. All feudal tenure is abolished by the Abolition of Feudal Tenure etc. (Scotland) Act 2000.

Feuar.

See **Vassal**.

Fiar. (pr. "fee-ar")

In the creation of a liferent and fee, the owner of the fee. See **Liferent**.

Fiduciary.

A person in a position of trust such as a trustee (as compared to a beneficiary) or company director who must not derive any undisclosed or unauthorised profit or advantage from his position.

Filiation (or **affiliation**).

The determination by a court of the paternity of a child, usually an illegitimate child sometimes described as *filius nullius*.

Fire-raising.

Setting fire to property, either wilful—in which case equivalent to the English crime of arson—or negligent or accidental.

Firm.

Besides its meaning of a partnership, this word also means the partnership or firm-name.

First instance.

A court of first instance is that which hears a case initially as contrasted with an appellate court or court of appeal.

First offender.

A convicted person not having previously been convicted of a crime or offence.

First Minister.

The head of the **Scottish Executive**, appointed by the Queen on the nomination of the members of the Scottish Parliament. The First Minister, among other functions:

(i) appoints Ministers in the Scottish Executive (including the **Law Officers**) with the approval of the Queen and agreement of the Scottish Parliament;

(ii) nominates the Lord President, Lord Justice Clerk, other Court of Session Judges, sheriffs and sheriffs principle; and

(iii) is the Keeper of the Scottish Seal. See **Seal**.

Fiscal.

As an adjective, pertaining to the national revenue. As a noun, see **Procurator fiscal**.

Fitted accounts.

Accounts between parties who have had business transactions, rendered by one and docqueted as correct by the other without any formal discharge. This puts the onus of proving that some amount is still outstanding upon the person so claiming.

Fittings.

Moveable articles temporarily attached to or connected with heritable property, e.g. carpets or curtains. See **Fixtures**.

Fixed charge.

A security affecting a particular property, e.g. a standard security over a house, as opposed to a floating charge.

Fixtures.

Articles in themselves moveable but so attached or connected to heritable property as to become part thereof, e.g. washing machines or sinks. See **Fittings**.

Flagranti crimine (or *flagranti delicto*).

Caught in the act of committing a crime. *Flagranti delicto* in modern terms can be used to refer to being caught in the act of committing a civil wrong.

Floating charge.
A security created by a company on all or part of its assets, permitting the assets to be dealt with and disposed of in the normal course of business until the charge crystallises and becomes fixed and enforceable by action of the creditor having a receiver appointed, or by the company's liquidation. In either case all the assets covered by the floating charge at the time of crystallisation are captured.

Force or fear (*vis aut metus*).
The Scottish technical terms for duress (the English term) or coercion, rendering an obligation void or voidable. A mitigating factor in criminal law.

Force majeure.
Something beyond the control of the contracting parties preventing performance of the contract.

Foreclosure.
A remedy of a security holder (usually a bank) involving taking over ownership of the security subjects from the defaulting debtor.

Forehand rent.
Rent payable by agreement in advance of the legal term of payment. See **Backhand rent.**

Foreign jurisdiction.
See *Renvoi.*

Forensic.
Generally, of or used as evidence in courts of law, e.g. forensic science, forensic medicine.

Foreshore.
See **Seashore**.

Forisfamiliation.
The departure of a child from the family on setting-up on his or her own account or marrying.

Forthcoming (or **furthcoming**).
See **Arrestement and furthcoming**.

Forum.
The court or tribunal appropriate for a particular purpose, the term *forum non conveniens* being applied to a court which although having jurisdiction is not the appropriate court for the matter in issue.

Fraudulent preference.
See **Gratuitous alienation; Unfair preference**.

***Fructus*: fruits.**
As a legal term includes fruit proper and also grain. *Fructus pendentes* are fruits not gathered. *Fructus percepti*, fruits that have been gathered. *Fructus civiles* are civil fruits, e.g. the rents and profits arising from

subjects producing no proper or natural fruits, such as rents of lands or houses or interest on money.

Fuel, feal and divot.

The name of a servitude giving a right of cutting peat and turf, for which feal and divot are Scots equivalents. See **Servitude**.

Fugitive offender.

A person apprehended in one part of the United Kingdom for return to stand trial in another part where he is accused of a crime or offence.

Full Bench.

A sitting of the High Court of Justiciary consisting of more than the **quorum** required for the hearing of criminal appeals generally (e.g. five, seven or nine).

Functus officio.

Having discharged one's official duty. Applies to a party such as an agent who has performed his duty and exhausted his authority, or to a judge or arbiter to whom further resort in the particular case or matter is incompetent.

Fund *in medio*.

See **Multiplepoinding**.

Fungible.

Fungibles are moveable goods meant for consumption (e.g. food) as opposed to non-fungibles meant for use but not consumption.

Furthcoming.

See **Arrestment and furthcoming**.

Furth of.

Outside the borders of, e.g. an action may be described as taking place "furth of Scotland".

G

Gable.

See **Mutual gable**.

Game.

A term covering a whole category of wild animals such as rabbits, deer, pheasants and grouse commonly killed for sport and/or food, the right to kill and take them being incidental to the ownership of land but subject to numerous statutory restrictions sometimes termed the Game Laws, regulating, for example, the seasons in which certain species may be hunted.

Gaming.

Playing games of skill or chance for stakes originally wholly illegal and now strictly controlled by statute; civil obligations contracted in such activities have always been legally ineffective. See *Sponsio ludicra*.

Gazette.

The *London Gazette* is the official government news sheet in which advertisements or intimations required by statute or court order have in some cases to be inserted for private interests. The Scottish equivalent is the *Edinburgh Gazette*.

General Assembly (of the Church of Scotland).

The highest court of the Church of Scotland, sitting annually and presided over by the Moderator.

General disposition (or **General conveyance**).

A deed which is a conveyance but lacks the pre-requisites for **infeftment**, e.g. a proper description of the land. This can arise for example, in a will or upon bankruptcy. Title is usually completed by registering a notice of title. See **Notice of title**.

General service.

See **Service**.

Gift.

In its normal sense, synonymous with donation, signifying gratuitous transfer by one person to another; it is also applied to the benefit represented by a bequest in a will and again to certain grants by the Crown, e.g. from a deceased's property acquired by the Crown as *ultimus haeres*.

Glebe.

Land to the use of which a minister in a landward parish has a right, over and above his stipend.

Good faith.

An act is done in good faith or **bona fide** if done honestly although mistakenly or sometimes even negligently or foolishly. An act is not in good faith if done fraudulently or deceptively or without inquiry where reasonable suspicion was raised. A person not in good faith is therefore in bad faith, or *mala fide*.

Grant.

The word denotes an original disposition and also a gratuitous deed; otherwise it generally has the same meaning as dispone.

Grassum.

A single payment made in addition to or in lieu of a periodic payment such as rent or feuduty.

Gratuitous.

Made or granted without payment or other consideration.

Gratuitous alienation.

The transfer of ownership of rights, goods or money by an insolvent debtor to another in the form of a gift (or, if a purchase, at a vastly inflated price). A gratuitous alienation is reducible either at the instance of creditors or of the trustee in sequestration. See **Unfair preference; Fraudulent preference**.

Ground annual.

A non-feudal duty on heritable property, payable annually. Their creation has been prohibited since 1974.

H

Habile. (pr. "hay-bile")

Admissible or competent for a legal purpose.

Habili modo.

In the manner competent.

Habit and repute.

(i) In criminal law the reputation of being a thief, the words being used in aggravation of the particular charge. Obsolete.

(ii) In civil law the reputation of being married that, coupled with cohabitation, constitutes a valid form of an irregular marriage. See **Irregular marriage**.

Haereditas iacens.

The property of a deceased person as existing between the moment of death and the confirmation of an executor in whom it vests retrospectively with effect from the death.

Hamesucken. (pr. "haim-suck-en")

An assault committed upon a person in his own house. Once a capital offence and still an aggravated form of assault particularly if accompanied by robbery.

Haver. (pr. "haav-er")

A person having documents in his possession that are required as evidence in a litigation.

Hearsay evidence.

Statements by a witness in court based on what he has been told by someone else and not based on his own direct observation, senses or knowledge. hearsay evidence is generally incompetent as evidence subject, however, to what are now broad exceptions. It is now almost always admissible in civil proceedings. In criminal proceedings the rule is more strenuously observed subject to a number of common law and statutory exceptions.

Heir.

(i) The person who succeeds to the property of a person deceased, whether by force of law or by express provision.

(ii) Until 1964, in a stricter sense (as often signified by the use of the term "heir at law") the person entitled under rules based on *primogeniture* and male preference to succeed to the deceased's heritable property (as distinguished from the heirs *in mobilibus*, being next of kin entitled to his moveable property). The meaning of the term in this context is lent greater precision by appending other words, e.g. heir-apparent, strictly an English expression meaning one who is bound to succeed X if only he survive him; *heir-female*, one of either sex who succeeds through a female; *heir-male*, the nearest heir who is a male and who is related solely through males; *heir-presumptive*, one who is nearest heir at a given moment but whose right may be ousted by the birth of one nearer; *heir of provision*, one who succeeds by virtue of express provisions as in a settlement; *heir of entail*, one entitled to succeed to entailed lands, so called, too, even after succeeding; and *heirs-portioners*, under the former law females succeeding *pro indiviso* to heritage to which there was no male heir.

Heritage.

The technical term for property in the form of land and houses, because it passed under the pre 1964 law to the heir on the owner's death. Whence the epithet heritable, as in heritable securities (e.g. heritable bonds), sums of money secured to the creditor over land. See **Heir**.

Heritor.

Strictly, any landowner, but in practice usually applied to a landowner in his role as a person liable to contribute to the upkeep of the parish church under the rules in force prior to the statutory reorganisation of church property and financial arrangements in 1925.

High Court.

See **Justiciary**.

Hinc inde.

Meaning "on either side". A good Latin phrase used frequently with such words as "claims", meaning the reciprocal claims made on one side and on the other.

Holding.

(i) Tenure in a feudal sense, as in blench-holding, ward-holding, feu-holding, and others.

(ii) Land held under a lease for agricultural purposes. See **Agricultural holding**.

Holding out.

By words or actions conveying the impression of a certain status or degree of authority, e.g. agent or partner. A person so holding himself out may thereby incur personal liability.

Holograph.

A document written wholly or as to all essential words in the handwriting of the grantor or signatory and thus valid and effective without the signature being witnessed. A typed deed could be "adopted as holograph" if these words were written by the signatory in his own hand. Holograph writings do not require any formality of signature and may be signed by the signatory according to their normal practice, e.g. a letter containing a testamentary intention, written in the signatory's handwriting and signed "mum" was, if separately proved to be the signatory's normal method of signing, holograph. Prior to 1995 certain deeds could only be valid if either attested (witnessed) or holograph. Holograph writings now have no particular status. They are not probative. See **Probative**.

Homicide.

The act of taking the life of another. See **Culpable homicide; Casual homicide; Murder**.

Homologation.

Prior to 1995, the act by which a party approved or confirmed a deed, contract, trust or other obligation (written or otherwise) that was otherwise defective. The effect of homologation was to validate the obligation from the date of its inception. Since 1995, the rules of homologation, and *rei interventus* have been replaced by the following statutory rule barring the withdrawal of a party where:

(i) there is a contract, obligation or trust not constituted in a written document;

(ii) one of the parties acted or refrained from acting in reliance thereon;

(iii) the acting or refraining from acting was within the knowledge and acquiescence of the other party;

(iv) the party who acted or refrained from acting has been affected to a material extent; and

(v) if there is a withdrawal from the original contract, obligation or trust the party who acted or refrained from acting would be adversely affected to a material extent. See *Rei interventus*.

Honorarium.

A monetary gift as a reward for services rendered: in theory applying to Counsel's fees that are not recoverable by any proceedings.

Horning.

An obsolete form of **diligence**. A creditor holding a court decree obtained *letters of horning* directing officers of the law to **charge** the debtor to pay: if the latter failed, the officer blew three blasts with a horn at the appropriate market-cross and then published the fact, which constituted *denunciation at the horn*. The defender became a rebel and was subject to *single escheat*, i.e. forfeiture of his moveables to the Crown. The same result was obtainable by registration of the decree with an executed charge in the Register of Hornings, which still exists.

Hypothec.

A right in security over effects of a debtor, valid without possession by the creditor, e.g. the landlord's hypothec for rent, the superior's hypothec for feuduty and certain maritime liens.

I

Illiquid.

Of an amount not yet fixed or ascertained. The opposite of liquid.

Impeachment.

(i) A special defence accusing another of the crime charged, otherwise known as incrimination.

(ii) Formerly a prosecution of an offender by the House of Commons in a trial in the House of Lords.

Impetrate. (pr. "im-pe-trate")

Procure or obtain perhaps by improper means.

Impignoration. (pr. "im-pin-yor-ation")

Pledging or pawning.

Implement.

To fulfil or carry out, as of duty, promise or contract.

Improbation.

A proving of a document false or forged as by the action of improbation.

Improbative.

Not probative. See **Probative**.

Improvements.

Meliorations other than normal repairs to leased subjects that, if carried out by the tenant may, particularly in the case of agricultural subjects, entitle him to compensation from the landlord at the termination of the tenancy.

In camera.

An English term referring to court proceedings conducted behind closed doors as opposed to being open to the public in accordance with the general rule.

Incapax.

As applied to a person, signifies legal, mental or physical incapacity.

Incest.

The crime represented by sexual intercourse between persons within the forbidden degrees of relationship, e.g. father and daughter, brother and sister. Now regulated by statute, incest includes relatives of full or half blood and also extends to adopted persons.

In chief.
Examination of a witness in court by or on behalf of the party calling him as opposed to his cross-examination by or on behalf of another party.

Incompetent.
An action is incompetent when the conclusions (e.g. the demand for a remedy) conflict with a rule of law applicable in the circumstances. For example, in Scotland it is considered incompetent to obtain an interdict against the Crown. See **Relevant**.

Incorporation.
The formation of a legal entity distinct from the constituent members, e.g. a public or private limited company.

Incorporeal.
As applied to heritable or moveable property, signifies something that has no physical existence, e.g. patent rights copyrights or a coat-of-arms.

Incumbrance.
See **Encumbrance**.

Indemnity.
An undertaking by one party to protect another from loss or injury arising in certain circumstances.

Indenture.
A form of contractual document variously used in English practice but in Scotland generally confined to apprenticeship or traineeship agreements, the name being derived from the shape in which the pages of the document were formerly cut.

Independent contractor.
A person engaged by another to perform some work or provide some service but not coming under the directions of the latter as an employee for whose actions there could be vicarious liability to third parties. See **Vicarious liability**.

Indictment.
An accusation of crime running in the name of the Lord Advocate and tried by jury in the High Court or Sheriff Court.

Induciae.
The period of notice allowed for his appearance granted to a person served with legal process. Commonly treated as a singular noun.

Industrial.
Brought about by the industry of a man as, e.g. industrial fruit crops, which means crops sown by man, not growing wild.

Infeftment.
The symbolic act of putting a person into possession of heritage and so completing his title, formerly by symbolically giving sasine or

possession by delivery of earth and stone; for long superseded by the equivalent consisting of the recording of deeds in the Register of Sasines or the Land Register of Scotland.

Infer.

Essentially an act of common sense, it is to deduce a conclusion (factual or legal) by a process of reasoning from the existence of one or more other facts. In lay usage only a person infers, but in legal usage a course of conduct could, for example, infer a penalty.

In foro.

As applied to a decree of the court, it signifies that decree has been granted against a party for whom appearance has been entered and defences or answers have been lodged, as opposed to decree in absence. A **decree** obtained by a pursuer *in foro* constitutes **res judicata**, while a decree in absence does not.

Ingather.

To collect or get in money or property due; used of executors, trustees, and the like.

In gremio.

Within the body of a document, e.g. a clause in a deed.

Inhibition.

A form of diligence which prevents a debtor from burdening or disposing of heritable property to the prejudice of the creditor inhibiting. Inhibition is personal, and applies only to the person inhibited. See **Adjudication; Arrestment and furthcoming; Attachment**.

In hoc statu.

In this state of matters; at this stage.

Initial writ.

The document by which proceedings in the sheriff court are normally initiated, the corresponding document in the Court of Session being the summons.

Injuria.

A legal wrong, i.e. an obligation created by operation of the law and not by consent.

In limine.

In court proceedings, means at the outset or initially; as applied to a proposition or argument put forward as early as possible once litigation has commenced.

In litem.

In the case or action.

In meditatione fugae.

Meaning "intending to flee the country". In an action by a pursuer against a defender for payment of a future or contingent debt, it constitutes a ground for obtaining the diligences of:

(i) arrestment on the Dependence of an action; or

(ii) inhibition. A separate ground of *vergens ad inopiam* meaning "nearing insolvency" is similarly available. See **Meditatione fugae warrant; Vergens ad inopiam.**

Inner House.

The two appellate divisions of the Court of Session, named the First and Second Division respectively (although other divisions often sit and are referred to as "Extra Divisions"). It is so-called originally on the simple topographical ground that their courts lay further from the entrance to the courthouse than did the Outer House.

Innominate contract.

Prior to 1995, a contract not falling within one of the well-known and named classes of contracts, which if also *unusual* required to be proved by writing or oath of the party.

In personam.

Describes a right or claim against a specific person only, e.g. a debt; as contrasted with a right *in rem*. See **Jus ad rem.**

In rem (jus in re).

Describes a right prevailing against other persons generally, e.g. a right of ownership.

In rem suam.

An adverbial phrase meaning to one's own advantage.

In rem versum.

An adjectival phrase meaning turned to one's own account.

In retentis.

Literally, amongst things kept for record: evidence is taken to lie *in retentis* when taken before the regular hearing of a case, where otherwise there is a risk of its being lost, e.g. due to old age, or emigration.

In solidum.

For the whole sum as where several obligants for a sum are each liable to the creditor for the whole.

Insolvency.

The state of being unable to pay one's debts:

(i) as they fall due; or

(ii) at a particular date, total assets being insufficient to meet total liabilities. See also **Apparent insolvency.**

Insolvency practitioner.

A person, usually an accountant or solicitor, qualified in terms of the Insolvency Act 1986 to act as liquidator or supervisor in relation to a company or as trustee or supervisor in relation to an individual.

Instance.

The part at the beginning of a summons or writ in which the parties to the action are identified.

Institute.

The person first named or called in a destination of property; those who follow upon him are substitutes. A "conditional institute" is one where the institution of a person is made contingent upon certain events.

Institutional writings.

The works of certain authors (generally in the seventeenth, eighteenth and nineteenth centuries) such as Stair, Hume and Erskine modelled on the Roman Institutes of Justinian, and dealing systematically and at length with the whole civil or criminal law. A statement in an institutional work is as authoritative as an appellate decision of the Court of Session.

Instruct.

(i) To vouch or support using a document or object.

(ii) To engage a professional person such as an advocate or solicitor to provide certain services.

Instrument.

A formal document creating or confirming some legal rule, right or liability. Throughout the UK statutory instruments are a standard form of subordinate or delegated legislation, while in former Scottish practice the term was frequently encountered in documents such as instruments of sasine and notarial instruments executed by notaries public.

Instrument of Resignation.

In feudal law, the deed by which a **vassal** returned his interest in land or property to the superior on a permanent basis (*ad remanentiam*) or singularly to another (*ad favorem*).

Inter alia.

Among other things.

Inter alios.

Among other persons.

Interdict.

The judicial prohibition issued by a Scottish court, comparable with the English injunction. In an emergency, *interim interdict* can be obtained on application **ex parte**.

Interim.

As applied to the ruling of a court, temporary or partial, as for example in matters of interdict, aliment, possession or expenses.

Interlocutor.

Strictly, in a civil action, an order or decision of the court short of the final judgment, but in practice applied to any order of the court.

Interlocutors are signed by the presiding judge and then entered on interlocutor sheets, being documents forming part of the process.

Intermeddle.

To interfere improperly or without any right.

Interrogatories.

Written questions adjusted by the court, to be put to witnesses examined under a commission.

Interruption.

The word is used of certain acts legally required in order to stop the running of a period of prescription.

Inter se.

Between or among parties themselves.

Inter vivos.

Between or among living persons: used of deeds meant to take effect during the granter's life as distinguished from deeds *mortis causa*, which only take effect on death.

Intestacy.

The position arising when a person dies intestate, i.e. without leaving a will. In the case of intestacy succession is governed by statutory rules. See **Testate**.

Intra vires.

Within the powers of a body such as a limited company or local authority. See **Ultra vires**.

Intrinsic.

See **Extrinsic**.

Intromit with.

To handle or deal with, as funds or other property: whence intromission; intromitter. If unauthorised, the action is *vitious intromission*.

Intrusion.

The delict of entering on possession of heritable property without violence but without any right.

Invecta et illata.

Effects brought on to premises, usually the effects of a tenant. The words appear to be pure synonyms.

Inventory.

A list, as of the property of a person deceased, that must be sworn to and lodged by executors on taking up their duties.

Inventory of process.

An inventory of the documents in a process that must be lodged in court along with them. So, too, there is an inventory of productions.

Investiture.

The progress or series of titles, by which a real right in lands is vested in the proprietor. See **Infeftment**.

I.O.U.

A contraction for "I owe you"; a document containing this contraction signed by the debtor is accepted as admission of his indebtedness to the holder or recipient in the amount of money therein stated.

Ipso facto.

By the fact itself.

Irregular marriage.

A marriage perfectly valid but carried through without the intervention of ecclesiastical or civil authority. There were originally three forms:

(i) declaration *de praesenti*, requiring only a genuine exchange of consent to marriage there and then;

(ii) promise *subsequente copula*, where sexual intercourse permitted in reliance of a promise of future marriage raised a rebuttable presumption that consent to marriage had thereby been obtained; and

(iii) cohabitation with habit and repute. Since 1940, only the third remains valid.

Irrelevant.

The opposite of relevant.

Irritancy.

The forfeiture of a right in consequence of neglect or contravention. It may be legal (implied by law) or conventional (the result of agreement). See **Clause**.

Ish.

Termination date (issue), commonly of a lease.

Issue.

(i) The formal question put for decision to a jury in a civil case.

(ii) A term covering all direct descendants of a person, not only his children.

Iter. (pr. "eater", or "itter" as in "hitter")

A rural servitude allowing one to pass over the land of another on horse or on foot; also known as "way". See **Servitude**.

J

Jedge and warrant.

An authority to repair or rebuild ruinous houses and to constitute the expense a real burden on the property given by the Dean of Guild prior to the disappearance of that body in the reorganisation of local government in 1975. Now obsolete.

Joint adventure (or **venture**).

A partnership for one particular transaction or commercial purpose.

Joint and several obligation.

A joint and several (or conjunct and several) obligation is one in which there is an obligation resting upon more than one person and each is liable for performance jointly with the others but also severally or individually. Several liability is where each obligant is singly liable to perform the whole obligation if called on; and the obligants are said to be liable *singuli in solidum*. The creditor can therefore sue all or any one of the debtors. See *In solidum*; **Joint obligation**.

Joint obligation.

An obligation binding several, yet each only for a share.

Joint property.

One of two modes in which a number of persons may concurrently have rights of ownership in the same subjects, the other being common property. In joint property the interest of a deceased owner passes by survivorship to the others and not to the deceased's representatives, as happens with common property. See **Accretion**.

Joint stock company.

A business entity with its stock or capital contributed by a number of persons, being the organisation now represented by the modern limited company.

Joint wrongdoers.

Two or more persons whose respective acts have caused injury or damage for which they are accordingly liable—jointly and severally.

Judicatum solvi.

Caution *judicatum solvi* is an undertaking that a sum of money found due by the court will be paid.

Judicial examination.

(i) The first appearance of a person charged with a serious crime when he may, if he wishes, make a declaration. Judicial examination takes place in the sheriff court before a sheriff and is conducted by a **procurator fiscal**.

(ii) The questions that may by statute be put to the accused by the Procurator fiscal at that appearance.

Judicial factor.

A person appointed by the court as an officer with the powers of a trustee to administer property in dispute or lacking adequate control and administration, e.g. as *curator bonis* on the estate of a person missing or of unsound mind or as factor on a trust or partnership estate.

Judicial reference.

In the course of a litigation, a reference of part or all of the matter in dispute to a referee, mediator or arbiter. Such a reference is made by agreement of the parties to the litigation together with the approval of the court.

Judicial review.

A remedy whereby the Court of Session may review and if necessary rectify the decision of inferior courts, tribunals and other public officers and authorities where no other form of appeal is available.

Judicial sale.

A sale under the authority of the court in various circumstances, as for example by public auction of effects subject to an attachment (previously a poinding) or in certain cases of property comprised in a heritable security. See **Attachment**.

Judicio sisti.

A form of caution in which the cautioner binds himself that the principal shall appear at all court diets to answer a civil claim or criminal charge. In the case of failure to appear the cautioner becomes liable for the amount contained in his bond of caution.

Jurisdiction.

(i) In international law the power of the state to enact and enforce legislation.

(ii) In national systems the power of a court to entertain particular cases as determined by factors such as location, district, status of the juristic or natural persons involved or the value or type of the cause.

(iii) The territorial area over which a particular court can exert its power; e.g. The Court of Session has jurisdiction throughout Scotland; a sheriff court has jurisdiciction in the sheriff court district.

Jurist.

A legal writer, scholar or philosopher.

Juristic person.

An artificial entity with legal capacity, rights and liabilities, e.g. an incorporated company, as distinct from a natural person.

Jury.

A group of lay persons chosen from the general public to decide upon issues of fact in legal proceedings. The decision of the members of a jury is confined within the scope of the directions on law that the presiding judge sets out in his **charge**. In Scotland a jury of 15 can reach a verdict in criminal trials unanimously or by a simple majority of at least eight. Civil jury trial is also competent in Scotland and such a jury is comprised of 12.

Jus ad rem.

A right to claim a thing singularly from or against the debtor in an obligation (it is thus also a *jus in personam)* but not to claim it as against all the world; the latter of which is "*jus in re*" and is a real right, a right in an item of property itself. The distinction between *jus ad rem* and *jus in re* is also often made by referring to them respectively as "personal" and "real".

Jus crediti.

A right vested in a creditor, not necessarily of instant payment.

Jus in personam.

See **Jus ad rem**.

Jus in re.

See **Jus ad rem**.

Jus in re aliena.

A real right (*jus in re*) held in the property of another: for example a standard security held by a lender, a servitude or a lease. Rights *in re aliena* are also referred to as subordinate real rights.

Jus quaesitum tertio.

A contractual right of one party, A, arising out of a contract between X and Y, to which A is not a party. The right arises as a consequence of a specific stipulation in the contract in A's favour.

Jus relictae.

The widow's right to one-third or one-half of her deceased husband's moveable property, according as there are or are not children or grandchildren. The right is calculated after deduction of debts and expenses, and any statutory rights if the deceased died intestate.

Jus relicti.

The widower's right comparable to *jus relictae*.

Jus tertii.

The right of a third party in an action. Where any person in a civil action advances arguments which he has no title or interest to maintain he may be met by the reply that such pleas are *jus tertii* to him. See **Jus quaesitum tertio**.

Justice-Clerk, Lord.

The second in dignity of the Scottish judges, who presides over the Second Division of the Court of Session. The title, like that of the Master of the Rolls, points to his comparatively humble beginnings as a clerk of court. See **Inner House**.

Justice, College of.

See **College of Justice**.

Justice-General, Lord.

The highest criminal judge in Scotland, presiding over The High Court of Justiciary. The position is, in modern times, held by the Lord President. See **Justiciar**.

Justices of the peace.

Lay persons appointed by the Scottish Ministers to preside as judges in the district courts, administer oaths and exercise other miscellaneous powers. See **District court; Stipendiary magistrate**.

Justiciar. (pr. "justice-ee-ar")

The ancient name, now obsolete, for the **Lord Justice-General**.

Justiciary, High Court of. (pr. "justice-ee-ar-ay")

The supreme Criminal Court of Scotland, consisting at present of 32 judges (Lords Commissioners of Justiciary) who are also the judges of the Court of Session. See **Circuit Court**.

Justifiable homicide.

Killing in exercise of a public duty as, for example, execution of sentence of death, or of a private right, as, e.g. of self-defence.

K

Kain (also **Cane**).

Animals or fowls, paid in lieu of feuduty or rent; virtually obsolete with the disappearance of payments in kind in feus and leases.

Keeper of the Records of Scotland.

The officer in charge of the Scottish Record Office wherein are preserved the public records of Scotland. See **Lord Clerk Register**.

Keeper of the Registers of Scotland.

The officer responsible for public registers including the Register of Sasines (see **Registration for publication**) and the Land Register for Scotland. See **Lord Clerk Register**.

Keeper of the Signet.

The titular head of the Society of Writers to the Signet, the effective head being the Deputy Keeper appointed by the Keeper.

Kindly tenant or rentaller.

A holder of land who, without having a feudal relationship with a superior, came to have a sort of hereditary right, usually constituted by entry in a landowner's rental book without any charter or other grant. The tenure has existed only in certain districts, notably Lochmaben in Dumfriesshire, and has in most cases been replaced by feudal tenure. Now abolished under the Abolition of Feudal Tenure etc. (Scotland) Act 2000.

Kirk-Session.

The church court that consists of the minister and elders of a parish.

L

Labes realis. (pr. "lab-es re-al-is")

An inherent taint or defect in a title to property, such for instance as affects stolen goods. Sometimes called ***vitium reale***.

Lacuna. (pr. "la-kyoon-a")

A gap or omission in a document, or a case not provided for in a statute.

Lammas.

One of the four quarter days in Scotland. Lammas was formerly the first day of August but is now by statute the 28th day of that month. See **Candlemas; Whitsunday; Martinmas**.

Landlord.

The proprietor of heritable property subject to a contract of lease, the other party being the tenant. See **Tenant**.

Land Register of Scotland.

The public register of interests in land in Scotland that under the system of registration of title progressively introduced under the Act of 1979 will eventually supersede and replace the Register of Sasines.

Land Tax.

A tax, otherwise known as **cess**, payable by landowners; latterly applying in Scotland only in country areas; now entirely extinguished as a result of redemption or exemption under statutory provisions.

Land tenure.

The basis or system under which land in Scotland is held of the Crown, the normal and main form being feudal tenure. Feudal tenure has been abolished as a result of the Abolition of Feudal Tenure etc (Scotland) Act 2000.

Lands Tribunal for Scotland.

A tribunal established by statute with jurisdiction in questions relating **inter alia** to the valuation of land, the discharge of restrictive land obligations, issues of disputed compensation for the compulsory acquisition of land, council house purchase disputes and complaints over non-domestic ratings assessments.

Lands Valuation Appeal Court.

A court comprising three Court of Session judges dealing with appeals from local valuation appeal committees.

Landward.

Prior to the local government reform of 1975 described areas lying outwith the burghs.

Last heir.

See ***Ultimus haeres***.

Law agent.

A common term (often shortened to "agent") for a solicitor or writer. The expression found statutory sanction in earlier legislation, but the tendency today is to substitute the English term "solicitor". See for example the Solicitors (Scotland) Act 1980.

Lawburrows.

An ancient but still competent process by which a person who apprehends danger to his person or property from another may have the other ordered by the court to find caution or security not to molest him.

Law Officers.

Government advisers on legal matters. In Scotland, the Law Officers of the **Scottish Executive** are the **Lord Advocate** and the **Solicitor General for Scotland**.

Law reports.

Reports of the decisions of the courts on disputed points of law published for the information of the legal profession and to be available where applicable as precedents in future cases; in Scotland they are now represented by the *Session Cases*, the *Scots Law Times*, the *Scottish Civil Law Reports* and the *Scottish Criminal Law Reports*.

Law Society of Scotland.

A body created by statute comprising all practising solicitors, controlling admission to and discipline within the profession (the latter through the Scottish Solicitors Disciplinary Tribunal).

Lay.

The term applied to persons not legally qualified but exercising quasi-judicial functions as for example on tribunals or acting as observers appointed to consider and report on complaints by members of the public concerning the legal profession.

Lead.

To "lead evidence" is to adduce or call evidence in the form of a witness. A "leading question" is one suggesting a certain answer from the witness to whom it is put. The term "leading case" is applied to a judicial decision regarded as an important precedent, while the senior counsel for a party in a case is sometimes termed the leader.

Legacy.

A gift, bequest or benefit derived by the legatee from the will of a deceased person.

Legal.

In addition to being used as an adjective, this word is used as a noun, meaning the 10-year period allowed by the law to a person whose property is in course of being adjudged, within which he may pay the debt and free the land of the adjudication. When *declarator of expiry of the legal* is pronounced the right to redeem is irretrievably lost. See **Adjudication**.

Legal aid.

Refers to the scheme set up by statute and operated by the Scottish Legal Aid Board providing representation or advice in matters civil or criminal for those the limits of whose means qualify them to be assisted persons, with or without liability to contribute to the expenses incurred.

Legal rights.

The claims which the surviving spouse and/or issue have to share in a deceased's estate whether or not he left a will; see *Legitim*; *Jus relicti*; *Jus relictae*; also **Terce** and **Courtesy**, the last two both being now abolished.

Legal tender.

The form in which a debt must be paid. In Scotland this comprises only coinage and Bank of England notes of less than £5, for which notes are no longer being issued. Scottish bank notes are not legal tender; however neither are credit cards, cheques or debit cards, all of which can be used as means of payment in the course of everyday transactions.

Legitim.

The part of a deceased's moveable estate to which his or her issue are entitled as a legal right, being one-third where there is a surviving spouse and one-half where there is not.

Legitimation *per subsequens matrimonium*.

The rendering legitimate of an illegitimate child by the subsequent marriage of his or her parents.

Lenocinium. (pr. "len-o-sin-i-um")

Furtherance by a husband of adultery committed by his wife. It constitutes a defence to an action of divorce by a husband on ground of his wife's adultery.

Leonina societas.

A form of partnership unrecognised in Scots law, in which one partner takes all the gain, the other bears all the loss. The term is sometimes applied to a partnership that is void or for some other reason illegal.

Lesion. (pr. "lee-shon")

Detriment, loss, or injury. When **enorm**, or considerable, a young person suffering it may have a transaction that is to his lesion set aside on the ground of minority and lesion.

Letters.

A **writ** or **warrant** issued by the court and under the signet. Procedure for a great variety of purposes was inaugurated by letters, but now only a few examples survive in practice, e.g. Letters of Inhibition as issued under the signet in the Court of Session.

Lex fori.
The law of the country in whose courts a litigation is taking place being the law regulating such matters as procedure and evidence in that litigation.

Lex loci actus.
The law of the place where the act in question was performed.

Lex loci contractus.
The law of the place where a contract was made or concluded, which is often the proper law by which to decide disputes about contracts.

Lex loci delicti.
The law of the place where the crime or delict in question was committed.

Lex loci rei sitae.
The law of the place where the subjects in question such as heritable property are situated.

Lex posterior derogat priori.
A rule of statutory interpretation meaning "a later law undermines an earlier law", i.e. if two statutes are inconsistent with each other, the later in date is presumed to prevail.

Libel.
In addition to its meaning of written defamation, this word also has the meaning of a criminal indictment. The verb to libel also bears both meanings, to defame in writing and to charge as a crime. See **Defamation**.

Licence.
(i) A permission from the appropriate authority to do something otherwise prohibited or restricted, e.g. the sale of intoxicating liquor.
(ii) A contractual right to the use or occupation of the heritable property of another not constituting a tenancy in the legal sense.

Licensing board.
A board comprising members of a district or island council who consider and determine applications for licences to sell alcoholic liquor.

Liege.
A subject of the Monarch or, as an adjective, one who is bound by feudal tenure.

Lien. (pr. "lee-en" or "lean")
The right to retain the property of a debtor until he pays, e.g. of a car mechanic to retain a car until the owner pays his garage bill. An English term now widely used in Scotland. See **Retention**.

Liferent. (pr. "life-rent")
Strictly, a *personal servitude* that entitles a man to the use, for his life, of another's property, though the liferenter's right is rather that of an owner for life. It is called a *proper liferent* when only **fiar** and liferenter

are involved; and an *improper liferent* when trustees are involved: it is a *legal servitude* when imposed by law (e.g. **terce**, though now abolished), and a *conventional servitude* when agreed; it is by reservation when the granter gives the fee but keeps a liferent, by constitution when he creates the liferent for another and keeps or disposes elsewhere of the fee. Liferent is often referred to as a *usufruct*, from the Roman law *ususfructus*, which conferred the right to use the subject and take the fruits or produce thereof. See **Servitude**.

Light and prospect.
A servitude binding the servient tenement, and preventing him from:
(i) building or planting on his ground (*non aedificandi*);
(ii) raising any buildings or plants on his ground beyond a certain height (*altius non tollendi*); or
(iii) building or planting so as to impinge on the light or prospect of the dominant tenement (*non officiendi luminibus*). In each of the three categories the servitude restrains the owner of the servient tenement in favour of the dominant tenement. See **Servitude**.

Limitation period.
Generally signifies the period within which court action in pursuit of a claim must be initiated, the term having particular reference to claims for personal injuries. Limitation is often confused with prescription. While prescription establishes or extinguishes rights themselves through lapse of time, limitation merely renders rights unenforceable by court action. See **Prescription**.

Limited liability.
The principle forming the basis of the modern limited company whereby liability of the shareholders for losses is limited to the amounts of their shares so far as unpaid. See **Shareholder**.

Lining.
Strictly the fixing or marking out of the boundaries of land. Formerly used in a wider sense to mean a decree of lining, i.e. the order of a **Dean of Guild**, authorising the erection or alteration of a building.

Liquid.
Of fixed and ascertained amount. A liquid debt is one ascertained and constituted against a debtor by written obligation or by judgment of a court. Liquidate damages means a sum of damages ascertained in advance inserted in a contract and exigible on a breach of the contract.

Liquidation.
The procedure for winding up and dissolving a corporate body such as a limited company, the person appointed to ingather assets and adjust and settle claims being called the liquidator.

Lis alibi pendens.
A plea taken by a defender to the effect that the action in which he is involved should not proceed because its subject matter is actually the

subject of litigation proceeding between the same parties in another court.

Litigious.

When land is rendered litigious it cannot be alienated to the effect of defeating an action or diligence that has commenced. Litigiosity results from inhibition and also from the service of the summons in certain actions affecting land.

Litiscontestation.

Joinder of issue in an action in court. In modern Scots law it arises on the lodging of defences after which any decree pronounced is a decree *in foro* as opposed to a decree in absence.

Local authority.

In Scotland a regional, district or island council elected by the inhabitants of the area in which it functions.

Locality.

A Teind Court decree, delimiting the amount of minister's stipend for which each heritor is responsible.

Local Valuation Appeal Committee.

A committee appointed by each local authority to deal with complaints affecting the assessment of heritable properties for business rating purposes.

Location.

Hire, whether of a person's services or of premises. The equivalent in Roman law is *locatio conductio* distinguished into various categories including: *locatio rei*, the hiring of a thing; *locatio custodiae*, the hire of the custody of a thing; *locatio operarum*, the hiring of service or the employment of work people; and *locatio operis faciendi*, the hiring of services to do a certain job, as in the employment of a contractor.

Lockfast place.

A room, cupboard, box or car, the breaking into which constitutes an aggravation of theft.

Loco parentis.

Applied to someone acting in place of a parent or in some way adopting the position of a parent.

Locum tenens.

A person acting as a substitute or deputy for another.

Locus.

The Latin word for a place, beloved of the police and certain lawyers in referring to the spot where an event of importance for the matter in hand took place.

Locus poenitentiae.

The opportunity to withdraw from a contract that is incomplete, or that is not binding on account of its informality: it is ousted by some form of personal bar as, e.g. *rei interventus*.

Locus standi.

The right to be heard before a tribunal or court. Also applied to the right to appear before a Parliamentary Committee in opposition to a Private Bill.

Lodge.

To lodge pleadings and other documents is to deposit them in the custody of the clerk of court. The English lawyer uses *file*.

Loose.

To remove, cancel, or take off, as, e.g. an arrestment.

Lord.

The proper title of address when speaking in court before a judge in the Court of Session and the High Court, or a sheriff in the Sheriff Court. It is correct to address the judge as "My Lord" or "Your Lordship" when speaking directly too him and "His Lordship" when speaking about the judge during proceedings (typically when speaking to a witness or addressing a jury). In Scotland, Senators of the College of Justice have only the honorific title "Lord"and are therefore not automatically members of the House of Lords. Female judges or sheriffs are addressed as "Lady" For this word in conjunction with others as in Lord President, see passim under the latter part of the title.

Lucratus.

A person is described as "*lucratus*" where he has become enriched in some way at another person's expense or as a result of another person's actions. The person "*lucratus*" therefore becomes liable, despite the absence of any contractual obligation, to compensate that other person to the extent that he himself has gained. The situation most commonly arises in the context of the law of unjustified enrichment. See *Quantum lucratus*; *Quantum meruit*; **Unjustified enrichment**.

Lyon King of Arms, Lord.

The principal administrative officer, who is also a judge, in Scottish heraldic matters and President in the Lyon Court.

M

Mace.

An ornamental staff of authority borne by a macer before a judge of the Court of Session and displayed in his court while it is sitting.

Magistrate.

Literally any person with judicial authority but in Scotland normally applied to provosts and bailies of burghs as formerly constituted and to stipendiary (i.e. salaried) magistrates functioning in certain criminal courts dealing with minor offences, but not to justices of the peace.

Mail or **maill.**

An obsolete word for rent, as in *grass mail*, the grazing rent for cattle. But it survives in the expression, *mails and duties*, an action of *maills and duties* being a form of diligence by which a heritable creditor procures the rents of the property to be paid direct to him. See **Blackmail**.

Major.

A person of full legal age, i.e. formerly 21 but reduced to 18 by the Age of Majority (Scotland) Act 1969. See **Minor**.

Mala fide ("in bad faith"); *Mala fides* ("bad faith").
See **Bad faith; Good faith**.

Malum in se.

"Bad in itself". This name is given to any wrongful act, the culpability of which arises from its being contrary to the laws of nature or rules of morality.

Male appretiata.

Wrongly valued; applied to the property of a deceased person, where a wrong valuation calls for a corrective inventory. In full the brocade is "*ad omissa vel male appretiata*", being things both omitted and/or undervalued. See *Eik; Omissa*.

Malice.

The preconceived intention to cause injury to another person. Recklessness is sufficient to constitute malice, since the legal meaning does not refer to malice in the sense of spite.

Malicious mischief.

The common law crime of damage to or destruction of property out of malice.

Man of skill.

The technical name for an expert in some particular subject to whom a remit may be made by a court for his report on some question arising in the case.

Mandate.

An authority given to one man to act (and strictly, to act gratuitously) for another, the former being termed mandatory and the latter mandant.

Mandatory.

Describes a requirement, e.g. in a statute which must be complied with and in respect of which a court has no dispensing power.

Manse.
The dwelling provided for a parish minister.

March.
Boundary; although common to both Scots and English this word is used with special frequency by Scots lawyers to describe the boundary between one property or estate and another.

Margin of appreciation.
In the interpretation of the text of the **European Convention of Human Rights**, the principle that each signatory state is entitled to a certain degree of latitude in resolving the inherent conflicts between individual rights and national interests.

Mark or **merk.**
An old Scottish silver coin, worth thirteen shillings and four pence scots.

Marriage-contract.
A contract entered into ante- or post-nuptially between persons about to be or actually married, for the purpose of regulating the rights in property of themselves and their children. Sometimes called a marriage-settlement, the English expression.

Martinmas.
One of the two term days in Scotland (the other being Whitsunday) as well as being one of the four quarter days. Martinmas was formerly the 11th day of November but is now by statute the 28th day of that month. See **Whitsunday; Candlemas; Lammas**.

Master and servant.
In modern parlance employer and employee, indicating a legal relationship under which one person engages another to perform work or provide services for him under his control.

Matrimonial home.
Any structure provided by one or both spouses and forming a family residence. See **Entitled spouse; Non-entitled spouse**.

Maxim.
A succinct statement of legal principle usually in Latin. See **Brocard**.

***Meditatione fugae* warrant.**
When a debtor was contemplating flight abroad, he could be apprehended and imprisoned in a limited number of cases on a *meditatione fugae warrant*. It has been incompetent since 1880.

Medium concludendi.
A ground of action on the basis of which a pursuer seeks a decree.

Meliorations. (pr. "me-lay-or-ations")
The technical expression for improvements to property made by such as a tenant or liferenter, the costs of which are irrecoverable from the **fiar** or **landlord**. Not much used.

Memorandum of Association.
One of the two essential and fundamental documents required for the incorporation of a company under statutory provision (the other being the Articles of Association); it includes specification of the company's objects and powers. See **Articles of Association**.

Memorial.
A document prepared by an instructing solicitor for counsel narrating certain facts and circumstances and indicating the question on which counsel's opinion is sought.

Mens rea.
Guilty purpose or criminal intent. See **Dole**.

Mercantile law.
The branch of law concerned with principles and customs affecting business, commerce and trade.

Mercy.
The royal prerogative whereby the sovereign may pardon a convicted person or cancel or reduce his sentence.

Merits.
A party to a litigation who has a claim or defence on the real matter in issue and not merely on some technical ground such as lack of jurisdiction is said to have a cause of action or defence on the merits.

Merk.
See **Mark**.

Messengers-at-Arms.
Formerly called Officers-at-Arms, are officers appointed by the Lord Lyon King of Arms, whose function is to execute civil and criminal process of the Court of Session and High Court of Justiciary. They are also sheriff officers and as such discharge similar functions for the sheriff court.

Messis sementem sequitur.
The occupier of land can reap the crops sown by him in good faith.

Mid-couples.
Statutes, decrees, deeds and other documents of title used or referred to in other documents as links, tracing an entitlement to heritable property in what is called a deduction of title.

Mid-impediment.
From the Roman law *medium impedimentum*, anything that intervenes between two events and prevents, in respect of the former event, the retrospective operation of the latter.

Minerals.
Materials below the surface of heritable property that will pass with a conveyance of the property unless reserved by the grantor.

Minor.
The term was formerly applied to a young person between 12 and 18 if female, 14 and 18 if male, but has sometimes been used in the wider sense of any person under 18 at which age since the passing of the Age of Majority (Scotland) Act 1969 full capacity subject to certain qualifications has been attained. Now however the Age of Legal Capacity (Scotland) Act 1991 has abolished the former two tier system of pupillarity and minority by giving children under 16 no legal capacity but those over that age full capacity subject to certain qualifications concerning matters arising before their attainment of majority at the age of 18. See **Nonage; Pupil.**

Minority and lesion.
See **Lesion.**

Minute.
(i) A record of a meeting.
(ii) A document forming part of a process by means of which a party (or parties, jointly) defines his position as to certain procedural matters as, e.g. by amending his pleadings, by referring to the oath of his adversary or by abandoning the action. In an undefended divorce it is applied to a document setting out evidence given on affidavit.
(iii) In a criminal trial, a document signed on behalf of the Crown and the accused agreeing facts which are not disputed.

Minute-book.
A book kept in the Register of Sasines in which are entered details, names of parties, date of presentation, etc. of deeds presented for registration.

Minute-book (of Court of Session).
A book in which are minuted or shortly stated, the heads of the judgments, that is of the acts and decrees pronounced by the Court or by Lords Ordinary.

Misdirection.
A mistake in law made by a judge in the course of his charge or legal directions to a jury.

Misfeasance.
Doing of an act (in an official capacity, e.g. a company director) in an unlawful manner.

Misrepresentation.
An untrue statement inducing the party to whom it is made to enter into a transaction or contract.

Missives.
A missive is a writing, usually in letter form. "Missives" is most frequently used in the context of the sale of heritage by private bargain (i.e. where the buyer offers to purchase from the seller and the seller accepts the offer). The letters may be written on behalf of the buyer and

seller by their solicitors. Completed missives (the letters of offer and acceptance taken together) constitute a contract binding on both parties for the sale of the heritage.

Mitigation.

Alleviation or melioration; the act of trying to make less severe. Best seen in the form of a "plea in mitigation" conducted by defence counsel following an accused person's conviction. The plea sets out to achieve the limitation, reduction or variation of the sentencing power available to the judge.

Mobbing and rioting.

The crime at common law where a group of persons act together for a common illegal purpose, which they effect or attempt to effect by violence, intimidation or a demonstration of force and in breach of the peace and "to the alarm of the lieges". It is also a crime to form part of a mob and no fixed number to constitute a mob is necessary.

Modification.

A Teind Court decree granting a certain stipend to a minister out of the teinds of the parish. See **Locality**.

Modify.

To reduce below the competent maximum, as expenses or a penalty.

Mora.

The delay in asserting a right or claim, that, when coupled with prejudice to the defender, may prevent the pursuer from succeeding.

Mortis causa.

On account of death: an instrument is made _mortis causa_ when it is intended to take effect after death; e.g. a will.

Mortgage.

An English term for a loan secured over property commonly applied in Scotland to loans on the security of heritable property.

Motion.

An oral or written application to the court made in the course of civil or criminal proceedings.

Motor Insurers Bureau.

An organisation established by insurance companies to deal with claims against parties who do not have the statutory third party insurance in respect of the vehicles causing damage or injury.

Mournings.

Mourning clothes, to which a widow and family have a legal right out of a man's estate, upon his death.

Moveables.

All property other than heritage. See **Corporeal; Incorporeal**.

Muirburn.

The seasonal burning of heather or similar growth that, with due care, a proprietor or occupier of land has a right to carry out.

Multiplepoinding.

An action by which property known as the "**fund *in medio***", whether heritable or moveable and claimed by different parties is brought into court either by the holder of the fund *in medio* (in which case the holder is known as the "real raiser") or by one of the claimants (in which case the holder is known as the "nominal raiser"), in order that the true ownership of, or respective rights to, the fund *in medio* can be determined all together in the same action. See **Double distress**.

Multures. (pr. "mooters")

The amount of grain that had to be given to the miller of a particular mill in return for his grinding the rest. **Thirlage** was a burden similar to a servitude by which land was formally astricted or thirled to a particular mill, to which grain had to be taken for grinding for payment of multures. "Dry multures" refers to duties paid in money or grain, whether the grain was ground or not.

Munus publicum.

A public office.

Murder.

The crime of homicide committed intentionally or with wicked disregard for the consequences of one's actions. See **Culpable homicide; Casual homicide**.

Murmur.

To murmur a judge is to defame him by imputing to him corruption, partiality, oppression or failure of duty.

Mutatis mutandis.

"Changing that which has to be changed"; or "with the necessary alterations", e.g. in a document or clause applying to various circumstances or contingencies.

Mutual gable.

In certain circumstances A may build an end wall of his house, as to half, over the boundary between him and the unbuilt land of X. If X builds he becomes the owner of that part of the wall resting on his land, with a common interest in the mutual gable, subject to paying one-half the cost of erection. See **Common interest**.

Mutuum.

A contract by which fungibles are lent without payment on the understanding that a like amount of the same will be restored at an agreed date.

N

Narrative.

The narrative of a deed sets out at the beginning the names of the grantor and grantee and the cause of granting. The English law term is "recitals".

Nasciturus.

Yet to be born. Rights may be conferred by law or by deed on those to be born in the future.

Naturalisation.

The conferring of nationality or citizenship of a country upon an alien of that country.

Natural justice.

The principles of fairness governing the conduct of courts, arbiters or tribunals in determining any dispute. Natural justice includes the principles that no man can be judge in his own cause, that each party is entitled to be heard and that justice is not only done but also seen to be done.

Natural persons.

Legal persons being human beings as distinguished from juristic persons such as corporations to whom personality is by law attributed.

Natural use.

In relation to heritable property its use for some normal purpose (e.g. agriculture) that apart from negligence does not infer liability for any resulting damage to other persons or their property; it is contrasted with unnatural use involving some innovation or alteration potentially dangerous and entailing liability for any resultant damage irrespective of negligence.

Nautae caupones stabularii.

Meaning "carriers by sea, innkeepers and stablers", the phrase is the name of the Roman Edict forming the basis of the liability for loss of or damage to customers' goods affecting parties such as inn or hotel keepers and common carriers irrespective of fault or negligence.

Negative prescription.

See **Prescription**.

Negative servitude.

See **Servitude**.

Negligence.

The absence of the care or diligence required by law, not to cause or permit harm to persons or not to breach the common law duty to take reasonable care in particular circumstances. Negligence has also been defined as "failure to exercise such care as is reasonable in all the circumstances to avoid damage to others and their property". Liability for negligence depends generally upon proof of three things:

(i) that the defender owed to the pursuer the duty to take care for the safety of the pursuer's person or property;

(ii) that the defender was in breach of that duty; and

(iii) that the breach caused damage to the pursuer's person or property. See *Culpa*.

Negotiable instruments.

Written obligations to pay money, e.g. bills of exchange including cheques and promissory notes, transferable by delivery or by endorsement and delivery without formal transfer, the **bona fide** transferee for value being unaffected by undisclosed defects of title. A Scottish banknote is a promissory note, and hence a negotiable instrument. See **Legal tender**.

Negotiorum gestor.

A person who, without any authority intervenes to manage the affairs of another who, temporarily or permanently, is unable to manage them himself, and in a situation where it is reasonable to assume that authority would have been given had the circumstances rendered it possible to apply for it. A gestor is entitled to be reimbursed for any expenditure he has incurred in the proper course of actings. The process is *negotiorum gestio*. See **Unjustified enrichment**.

Nemine contradicente (nem. con.).

Without dissent, applying to a proposition put forward by a number of persons without anyone opposing it.

Nemo dat quod non habet.

One of the most famous of latin maxims, meaning "no one can give what he has not got", it expresses the principle that one without legal title cannot grant legal title to another. The rule is more accurately stated in the maxim *"Nemo plus iuris ad alium transferre potest quam ipse haber"* meaning "no one may transfer more right [in a thing] to another than he has himself".

New trial (or re-trial).

In criminal trials or civil jury trials one or more re-trials (new trials) may be allowed on account of irregularities in the preceding trial or new matters arising since then.

Next-of-kin.

Prior to the Succession (Scotland) Act 1964, the class of relatives (not including a spouse) entitled to succeed to moveables at common law.

Nexus.

A bond, tie, fetter or connection, e.g. attaching to property or funds arrested or made the subject of a charge.

Nimious.

Stock epithet meaning vexatious or excessive, used in conjunction with oppressive in the expression *nimious and oppressive*. See **Oppression**.

Nobile officium.

The noble office or power of the Court of Session or High Court of Justiciary. It is strictly limited to the equitable jurisdiction of either court to modify the common law or give relief in a situation where no legal provision exists.

Nomen juris.

Meaning "legal term", or "legal name" i.e. of a word or words having a particular technical meaning in law as opposed to everyday usage.

Nominal raiser.

See **Multiplepoinding**.

Non aedificandi.

See **Light and prospect**.

Non compos mentis.

Of unsound mind.

Non officiendi luminibus.

See **Light and prospect**.

Non valens agere.

That a person was not fit to act, *non valens agere*, by reason of minority and the like, formerly prevented prescription running against him.

Nonage.

In civil law nonage now refers by statute to anyone aged under 16 (Age of Legal Capacity (Scotland) Act 1991). Nonage bars the validity of certain legal transactions, such as marriage or legal proceedings. The statute abolishes the distinction in civil law between pupillarity and minority. In criminal law, nonage refers to children under 8 years, who by statute cannot be guilty of any offence. See **Minor; Pupil**.

Non-entitled spouse.

A spouse with no right of ownership or otherwise in a matrimonial home but having the right of occupancy conferred by the Matrimonial Homes (Family Protection) (Scotland) Act 1981. See **Entitled spouse**.

Notarial execution.

The signing of a document by a notary public or other qualified person on behalf of a party blind or for some other reason unable to write.

Notarial instrument.

A narrative under the hand of a notary detailing procedure that has been transacted by or before him in his official capacity. As a form of completion of title to heritable property it has now been replaced by the notice of title.

Notary public.

A functionary known throughout European civilisation, before whom affidavits and other documents can be sworn. His duties in Scotland have been of great importance in recording transactions in land and in matters of shipping, bills of exchange, and bankruptcy. In Scotland a solicitor is admitted to the office of notary public by the Court of Session.

Note.

A step of Inner House proceedings in the Court of Session used for making an incidental application. Also, the part of a sheriff court judgment in which the reasons for the decision are given.

Notice of title.

A deed executed by a law agent or notary public showing how by deed or otherwise the right of a certain party to heritable property is constituted and completing his title to the property by being recorded in the Register of Sasines or Land Register. See **General disposition; Notarial instrument**.

Notice to quit.

A notice given by either party to a lease of heritable property indicating the intention to terminate the tenancy contract: if the notice comes from the tenant it is more appropriately described as a Notice of Intention to Quit.

Notour bankruptcy.

Formerly a state of insolvency as existing in circumstances prescribed by statute. Now replaced by apparent insolvency as the statutory prerequisite for the initiation by creditors of sequestration proceedings. See **Apparent insolvency**.

Not proven.

One of the three verdicts open to a jury or sheriff in a criminal trial in Scotland. It has the same effect as a verdict of not guilty, i.e. the accused is acquitted. However the distinction between not guilty and not proven could be described as a question of emphasis, not guilty being a more emphatic acquittal than not proven.

Nova debita.

A term used in bankruptcy law to describe debts incurred by the bankrupt in transactions involving reciprocal obligations. Although incurred by the bankrupt while insolvent their settlement is not challengeable as a fraudulent preference.

Novation.

The replacement, by agreement, of one obligation by another, the parties remaining the same.

Novodamus.

A charter of *novodamus* is used to make some change in the incidents of a feudal holding or to correct a mistake.

Nuisance.

An act or omission in breach of some rule of common law or statutory provision such as one affecting the occupation of heritable property, the act or omission causing damage, annoyance or inconvenience to occupiers of property or other persons. Thus the latin maxim "*sic utere tuo ut alienum non laeda*", "use your own property as not to injure that of another." This principle of Roman law contains the only restriction laid upon the otherwise unlimited right which a proprietor has of using his own property according to his own pleasure.

Nullity.

Non existent or lacking legal force as applied to acts or writings which are null and void: also applies to a marriage affected by an inherent defect such as existence of a prior marriage or relationship within a prohibited degree.

Nuncupative.

Oral, as contrasted with written: normally of a will. Latin, *nuncupare heredem*, to name an heir publicly before witnesses.

O

Oath.

An affirmation or denial or promise, attested by the name of God. In court proceedings it is the undertaking by a witness to give truthful evidence, the alternative for a witness having no religious belief being affirmation. Reference to oath is a form of proof in which a litigant requests his opponent to answer certain questions on oath with challenge or contradiction incompetent. See *De fideli*; **Calumny; Perjury**.

Ob contingentiam.

See **Contingency**.

Ob majorem cautelam.

As a precaution or for greater security.

Ob non solutum canonem.

On the ground of unpaid feuduty. Used of irritancy of a feu for this reason. *Canonem* is commonly mispronounced with the accent on the second syllable.

Obediential.

Used of obligations, meaning imposed by law in consequence of the relationship in which the parties are placed, as distinct from contract: e.g. a parent's obligation of **aliment** to his children; the duty of a person enriched at the expense of another to make recompense under the law of unjustified enrichment; or the delictual duty of a person at fault to pay damages to the person wronged. See **Conventional**.

Obiter dictum.

An opinion expressed by a judge in his judgment upon a point not essential to the decision of the case. See **Ratio decidendi**.

Obligant.

The debtor in an obligation. He is in English law the obligor and the creditor is the obligee, a term sometimes used in Scotland also.

Obligation.

The branch of law (also referred to as "actions") that deals with personal rights (rights *in personam*) enforceable between parties and usually involving a creditor and a debtor. The law of obligations deals with rights arising from promise (a "unilateral obligation"), contract ("bilateral obligation"), by operation of law (**delict**) or by the order of a court. It includes the law of **unjustified enrichment**. An obligation is thus a legally enforceable duty owed by own to another. See **Conventional; Obediential**.

Obligationes literis.

In present Scots law, *obligationes literis* are obligations that must be constituted in writing in order to have legal effect. The law is now governed by s.1 of the Requirements of Writing (Scotland) Act 1995, which sets out that certain contracts, obligations, trusts, conveyances and wills must be constituted in writing e.g. disposition of heritable property.

Obtemper.

To obey, usually of the decree or order of a Court.

Occupancy or *occupatio*.

A mode of acquiring a property by appropriating a thing, e.g. a wild animal, never before owned by anyone. Also the physical possession and use of heritable property.

Occupier's liability.

The duty of care required of the occupier of premises to those entering the premises as now regulated by the Occupiers Liability (Scotland) Act 1960 replacing the categories of invitee, licensee and trespasser originating in England but adopted in Scotland.

Offence.

A punishable act or omission contravening some rule of law, usually one contained in a statutory provision.

Officers of the State.

Historically the important officials of state in Scotland, namely the Lord Lyon, the Lord Justice-General, the Lord Justice-Clerk, the Lord Advocate, the Solicitor-General, the Keeper of the Great Seal, the Lord Clerk Register and the Lord High Constable.

Ombudsman.

An independent official appointed to receive and investigate complaints made by individuals against abuses or capricious acts of public officials. At UK level there is the right of complaint to the Parliamentary Ombudsman and the Health Service Ombudsman. In Scotland the right of complaint regarding any **devolved matter** is to the **Scottish Public Services Ombudsman**.

Omissa (*vel male appretiata*).

Things omitted from or erroneously valued in the confirmation of an executor, to remedy which a new grant, *ad omissa*, may be made. See *Eik*.

Oneris ferendi.

One of two Roman law servitudes falling into the category of urban support, the other being *tigni immittendi*. *Oneris ferendi* is the right of the dominant tenement to the support of buildings on it. See **Servitude**.

Onerous.

Granted for value or consideration, as distinguished from **gratuitous**. The noun is *onerosity*.

Onus.

The burden or responsibility of proving certain facts at issue in court proceedings commonly referred to as the onus of proof resting on one or other party.

Ope et concilio.

By help and counsel (strictly, *consilio*), a phrase comparable to **art and part**. Used occasionally, without much reason, by practitioners.

Ope exceptionis.

A plea that a document founded on in civil proceedings and concerning only the parties involved is null and void and should be set aside and disregarded. The plea is useful in the sheriff court where actions of reduction are incompetent.

Open account.

A debt entered in a book not constituted by voucher or decree.

Open exclusivity.

The quality of an agreement, such as a licence or assignation of an industrial or commercial property right, by which A agrees:
(i) to supply to B goods for retail in a particular geographical area and to no other person; and
(ii) not to compete directly with B in that area. Unlike **absolute exclusivity**, there is no agreement between A and B to prevent other persons from competing in the area in question.

Opinion.

(i) A statement, usually written, by an advocate or solicitor of his view on a matter on which he is consulted.

(ii) A statement by a court or judge setting out the reasons for the decision in a case: also applied to the decision in an appeal by stated case and to the decisions of the Court of Session. (*N.B.*: Sheriffs and Court of Session judges write opinions; English judges write judgements; House of Lords judges give speeches.)

(iii) As applied to evidence given in court the testimony of an expert on a matter in issue based on facts made known to him.

Oppression.

A crime consisting of partiality or refusal of justice by a judge, in the persistent bringing of groundless charges by an official prosecutor, or in any abuse of judicial position for personal reasons.

Opus manufactum.

Artificial works, in contrast to natural features e.g. dams to store water or earthworks to prevent flooding.

Order in Council.

A form of delegated legislation similar in effect to a statutory instrument consisting of a decree or order made by the sovereign with the advice of the Privy Council.

Ordinary action or cause.

Any civil proceedings in the Court of Session or Sheriff Court other than proceedings for which special procedure is provided in the rules of the Court of Session or Sheriff Court rules. Examples of special procedure in the Court of Session are Commercial cause, Personal Injury cause or Family actions. In the Sheriff Court, examples are Summary cause and **Small Claims procedure**.

Ordinary, Lords.

The judges, at present 32 in number, who try cases at first instance in the Court of Session.

Outer House.

The part of the Court of Session which exercises a first instance jurisdiction. See **Inner House**.

Outside plenishings.

Implements kept out of doors, as of husbandry.

Outwith.

Outside of, beyond, without.

Overriding interests.

Temporary or permanent rights such as tenancies or servitudes binding proprietors of land although not disclosed in either the General Register of Sasines or the Land Register.

Overrule.

Applies to the decision of a superior court declaring wrong and not authoritative the decision of an inferior court, whether in the same action or cited as precedent in a later case.

Oversman.

The person to whom falls the duty of deciding, when arbiters differ. In English law, umpire.

Overt.

An overt act is something done openly and publicly without concealment as distinct from some intention or act not so manifested.

Overture.

A formal proposal for a change of church law, made in the **General Assembly**.

P

Pactum de non petendo.

An agreement, absolute or temporary, that one party will not enforce his rights against another.

Pactum de quota litis.

An agreement (invalid in Scotland), by which a legal adviser agrees to accept part of what is recovered by the court action, in lieu of a fee. Such a fee is permitted in certain foreign jurisdictions.

Pactum illicitum.

Unlawful contract: use of the Latin is common.

Panel or pannel.

The accused person in a criminal action proceeding before a jury, from the time of his appearance, is styled the panel. See **Accused**.

Pari passu.

Frequently used by lawyers, meaning little if anything more than "share and share alike" or "ranking equally", e.g. in the case of claims or security rights.

Parliamentary Corporation.

See **Scottish Parliamentary Corporate Body**.

Parole.

A form of conditional release from prison before the expiry of a custodial sentence.

Parole evidence.

Oral evidence of witnesses, as contrasted with documentary evidence.

Pars judicis.

The "part or duty of a judge" that he must notice and act upon irrespective of the wishes of the parties, e.g. dismissing proceedings not within his jurisdiction.

Particeps criminis.

Latin for accomplice, occasionally used in writing and speaking.

Partner.
A person carrying on business in common with another with a view to profit and so constituting a partnership or firm.

Parts and pertinents.
Everything connected with or forming part of lands conveyed (except the *regalia)* that is not specially reserved from the grant as, e.g. the **solum** of a lake or a right of pasturage on other lands. See **Pendicle**.

Passim.
Meaning "throughout" or "frequently"this latin term is used to indicate that a particular word, term of phrase is used extensively throughout a text.

Passing off.
The actionable civil wrong involved in misleading the public into believing that a business or certain goods are those of someone other than the parties to whom they belong.

Passive title.
An expression which is used to denote the legal position of one (such as a vitious intromitter) who through interference with the property of a deceased person is held liable for his debts: in contradistinction to the *active title* of one who can take action to recover debts, having duly obtained confirmation as executor.

Pasturage.
A servitude that confers right on the holder of the dominant tenement of pasturing cattle or sheep on ground of the servient tenement. See **Servitude**.

Patent.
A monopoly right over an invention (i.e. incorporeal heritable property) granted for a specified period (now 20 years) by the Crown under statutory provisions.

Patrimony, Patrimonial.
The noun has been defined as "an hereditary estate or right descended from ancestors." The adjective has a wider sense meaning pertaining to property, of any kind. A patrimonial loss is a loss in respect of property (e.g. loss of wages, loss of pension rights), as contrasted with, say, bodily injury.

Pawn.
See **Pledge**.

Pejorations or deteriorations.
The contrary of **meliorations**.

Penal action.
An action in which are sought not merely ordinary damages but extraordinary damages by way of penalty. Penal damages are generally

not recoverable under Scots law, however procedure by Petition and Complaint provides an example.

Penal irritancy.

An irritancy in which the loss involved by exercise of the irritancy is disproportionate to the value of the right which is secured by it.

Pendente lite.

While an action is pending before the court.

Pendicle.

Usually encountered in the phrase *parts, pendicles and pertinents.* (See **Parts and pertinents**.) Pendicle means a small piece of ground, and also anything that is attached to another. It thus seems to extend somewhat the sense of parts and pertinents.

Penuria testium.

Lack of witnesses; its significance was that it sometimes justified the calling of witnesses, otherwise incompetent, in times when absolute disqualifications of certain parties as witnesses were commoner than now.

Per capita.

Equal division by heads among beneficiaries in succession. When a testator provides that his estate be so distributed, it is divided into as many shares as there are persons called to the succession. See *Per stirpes*.

Per stirpes.

Literally, equal division "by stocks" among beneficiaries in succession. The difference between it and division per capita is best shown by illustration: A grandmother leaves funds for her three grandchildren, two being the children of her son A, one being the child of her other son B. According to division per capita, the grandchildren would each receive one third of the funds; but by division *per stirpes* the fund would be halved first between the grandmother's two sons, meaning the two children of A would each receive one quarter of the funds while the child of B would receive a half.

Peremptory.

An epithet applied to the defences in an action, "*quae perimunt causam*", meaning "which destroy or put an end to the pursuer's case." A peremptory defence typically contains positive allegations that enter into the merits of the case itself, and have the effect of either taking away the ground of action, or of extinguishing its effects. See **Dilatory defences**.

Periculo petentis.

At the risk of the party seeking it, e.g. an interim interdict granted by the court on the statement of one party.

Per incuriam.

Through negligence, mistake or error.

Perjury.

The crime committed by a witness in court proceedings involving the affirmation of a deliberate falsehood on oath or on an affirmation equivalent to oath.

Per se.

In itself or alone.

Person.

The legal or natural entity capable of exercising rights (such as owning property, entering into agreements and raising court actions) or incurring liabilities, such as debt. Natural persons are individuals; legal persons include registered companies, partnerships, trusts and unincorporated associations (such as clubs).

Persona standi in judicio.

The right of all enjoying full rights of citizenship and who are **sui juris**, to pursue, vindicate and defend their rights in a court of law.

Personal bar or **personal exception.**

A plea taken by one party to litigation based on an assertion that the other party has so spoken or acted as to induce a reasonable belief in a particular state of affairs, upon the faith of which the party taking the plea has acted to his prejudice. That other party, if found to be "personally barred", is not permitted to refute the inference to be drawn from his words or conduct. The English term is estoppel. See **Homologation;** *Rei Interventus.*

Personal property or estate.

The English equivalent of **moveables**.

Personal right.

See *Jus ad rem.*

Personation.

Pretending to be another person: a crime at common law if fraudulently perpetrated.

Per subsequens matrimonium.

Legitimation of an illegitimate child as affected by the subsequent marriage of its parents.

Pertinents.

See **Parts and pertinents**.

Perversion of the course of justice.

Used in criminal charges to describe such actions as interference with witnesses or falsification of evidence.

Petition.

An **ex parte** application to the Court of Session for a purpose such as the grant of a special power or exercise of a particular jurisdiction. See **Summons**.

Petition and Complaint.

The procedure in the Court of Session where the remedy sought is a criminal or quasi-criminal one, as against officers of court for malversation (being misconduct in the discharge of a duty or trust).

Petitory action.

An action in which the court is asked to decree payment or performance by the defender to the pursuer in consequence of a right of property or credit held by the pursuer.

Pignus.

From Roman law, a pledge or the contract involving it. See **Pledge**.

Plagium. (pr. "play-gee-um")

The theft of a child below the age of puberty, the child's parents having a right of custody akin to a right in property of the child. In Roman law the theft of a slave.

Plead.

(i) To argue a case in court.

(ii) To argue a case on paper, as in the condescendence in an action; hence the expression "the pleadings" for the papers or record in a case.

Plea in bar of trial.

See **Bar**.

Plea in law.

A short proposition at the end of pleadings (e.g. a **Summons**, **Initial writ**, **Defences** or **Petition**) showing exactly the remedy sought and why, as a matter of law, it should be granted.

Plea in mitigation.

See **Mitigation**.

Pledge (otherwise **Pawn).**

The delivery of moveable property in security of an obligation. Where the property is money the pledge is referred to as **Deposit**.

Plenishing.

Moveable property such as furniture, stock or gear brought on to heritable property usually to furnish it.

Pluris petitio.

Asking in an action more than is due.

Poaching.

A statutory offence involving the unauthorised taking of game or fish from private property or in any location in which such activity is illegal.

Poind.
To take a debtor's moveables by way of execution (now obsolete). To *poind the ground* is to take the goods on land in virtue of a real burden possessed over the land. The word is pronounced *pind*. Poinding has been statutorily replaced by **Attachment**.

Policy.
The name generally given to the document constituting and defining the terms of a contract of insurance or assurance.

Policies.
The grounds in which a large house or mansion is situated.

Poors' roll.
A roll or list of the causes in which, under the system now replaced by legal aid, a party enjoyed free legal representation by solicitors and/or counsel.

Portioner.
In feudal law, the proprietor of a small feu. See **Heir**.

Possession.
Detention of a thing with the intention to hold it as one's own or for one's own benefit. It differs from custody, which is conditional and limited possession, held not for the custodier but for another.

Possessory action.
An action founded on possession and used for the limited purpose of holding or recovering possession.

Power of appointment (or **apportionment**).
The authority given to a person by a deed such as a will or **inter vivos** deed of trust for the disposal or division of property of the grantor in accordance with the directions of trustees or other parties.

Power of attorney.
A power given to X by A to act for him. An English term, but now much used, the true Scottish term being **factory** or **commission**.

Practicks.
Notes on decisions of the Court of Session compiled by members of the court: the precursor of the law reports.

Praecipuum.
A right which, being by its nature indivisible (as the right to a peerage) went to the eldest and not to all heirs-portioners jointly. See ***Primogeniture***.

Praedial. (pr. "pry-dee-al")
As applied to servitudes, means those affecting heritable property (from "*praedium*", meaning land or or real property). All servitudes affecting heritable property are called praedial and are often divided into rural and urban. See **Servitude**.

Praepositura.

The managership of a married woman in domestic matters (she was *"praeposita rebus domesticis"*), entitling her to pledge her husband's credit for necessaries, now abolished. *Praepositura* is also generally referred to as the office conferred by a principal on his factor, agent or servant, under which the latter is authorised to carry on the business of the former.

Precarium.

A loan that is given gratuitously and can be recalled at will, the term *precario* as used in various contexts meaning "at will". In the civil law *precarium* included everything that one had obtained from another by prayer or entreaty (*preces*). The person from whom the possession had thus been obtained could resume possession "at will" at any time under the action *de precario*; and hence the word *precarious* came to mean "uncertain".

Precatory.

The term applied to words in a will requesting or recommending but not actually directing that something be done. It is a question of construction whether such words are to be given mandatory effect.

Precedent.

(i) The decision of a court regarded as a source of law or authority in the decision of a later case.

(ii) A form of deed or writ regarded as basically satisfactory and accordingly suitable for use or adoption in legal practice. See, for Scotland, **Style**.

Precept. (pr. "pree-cept")

A warrant or authority formerly granted by a judge or other person having power in the circumstances; occurring in such expressions as *precept of arrestment, of clare constat, of sasine* (the warrant for infeftment of a vassal given by a superior to his bailie), *of poinding, of warning.*

Precognition.

A statement or record of the evidence a person may be expected to give if called as a witness in proceedings civil or criminal, as ascertained by his interrogation on behalf of a party or parties to the proceedings.

Pre-emption.

Formerly signified the clause in a feudal grant entitling the superior to the first offer should the vassal decide to sell the feu but now applies to a condition of that kind irrespective of the relationship of the parties to the deed containing it.

Prejudice.

(i) The phrase "without prejudice" as often used in the course of negotiations for settlement of a dispute implies that if settlement is not reached the negotiations are not to be referred to or founded upon in any way.

(ii) The phrase "without prejudice to" is used in statutes and documents in referring to matters or provisions not to be affected by the section or clause containing these words.

Preliminary defence.

Another name for **dilatory defences**.

Presbytery.

A church court next above the Kirk Session, consisting of a minister and elder from each church within a certain district.

Prescription.

The passing of a period of time that confers rights or that, regarded from another point of view, cuts off rights. *Positive prescription* creates rights, *negative prescription* extinguishes rights. The prescriptions now operating are the two positive prescriptions of 10 years and 20 years and four negative prescriptions of 2 years, 5 years, 10 years and 20 years respectively. There is some argument for the existence at common law of a 40 year acquisitive prescription of moveable property. See **Limitation**.

Presents.

In a deed "these presents" means the deed itself.

Preses. (pr. "praises")

Chairman, or person presiding at a meeting.

President, Lord.

The judge who is head of the Scottish judiciary, presiding in the First Division of the Inner House in the Court of Session and having various administrative powers and functions. The same judge in modern times holds the position of Lord Justice-General.

Presiding Officer.

Elected from among the members of the **Scottish Parliament**, the Presiding Officer's principal responsibility is to chair meetings of the parliament in the debating chamber. He is also chairman of the **Parliamentary Corporation**.

Prestation.

Performance of an obligation or duty; *prestable*, means payable, exigible, enforceable.

Presumption.

In the law of evidence an inference or conclusion that may be drawn from certain facts admitted or established.

Pretium affectionis.

A price or value placed upon a thing owing to its owner's attachment to it. The term is also used in connection with the right to insist on specific implement of a contract such as the sale of a particular article not otherwise obtainable.

Prevaricate.
To wilfully conceal or suppress the truth. If done while on oath it is usually dealt with as contempt.

Prima facie.
At first sight.

Primogeniture.
The principle whereby at common law the eldest male descendant inherited as heir at law the heritable property of a person dying intestate. Under the statutory provisions *primogeniture* and the preference of males over females with which it operated, no longer apply except to titles, coats-of-arms, honours or dignities transmissible on the holder's death.

Primo loco.
In the first place.

Primo venienti.
Literally first to come forward, e.g. as creditors of a deceased person more than six months after his death.

Prince of Scotland.
The title borne by the eldest son of the sovereign, the Principality comprising certain lands in Scotland from which he draws the revenues.

Principal.
The person for whom an agent or mandatary acts. See **Agent; Mandate.**

Prior rights.
The statutory rights of the spouse of a person dying intestate to the deceased's dwelling-house with furnishings and plenishings and a financial provision out of the remaining estate.

Private Act of Parliament.
A local or general Act passed under private legislation procedure giving special power or rights to a particular person, body or authority.

Privative jurisdiction.
Jurisdiction residing in one court to the exclusion of others. For example, the sheriff court has privative jurisdiction in civil actions craving £1,500 or less.

Privilege.
The legal right in certain circumstances to do or say something unrestricted and without liability, e.g. statements of a witness in court or of a member in Parliament.

Privileged debts.
Debts owed by the estate of a deceased, such as for funeral expenses and mourning, which take preference over the debts of ordinary creditors.

Privileged summons.

One in which, from the nature of the case, short *induciae* (i.e. period of notice) are allowed.

Privy Council.

The council of the sovereign that, through its judicial committee, exercises a judicial function in certain appeals. Since the Scotland Act 1998 it has been competent to appeal to the Privy Council in criminal cases involving an argument arising from the **European Convention on Human Rights**.

Probabilis causa litigandi.

Prima facie grounds for raising or defending civil proceedings. Such grounds required to be demonstrated by a party seeking to litigate on the (obsolete) **poors' roll** and are now required to obtain legal aid.

Probate.

The English equivalent of confirmation of an executor nominate; letters of administration being the equivalent of confirmation of an executor dative.

Probatio probata.

A fact given in evidence that may not be contradicted.

Probation.

(i) Proof in civil proceedings. See **Conjunct probation; Replication, Proof in**.

(ii) In criminal law a mode of treatment of offenders forming an alternative to imprisonment.

Probative.

Where the law requires formal execution in writing for certain transactions (such as for the sale of a house) a probative document is one that is "self-proving", and affords **prima facie** proof of its own contents. In any court proceedings a probative document is one that will be presumed to be validly executed. A document that is not probative would require to have its valid execution established by the party seeking to rely upon it. Since 1995 a document is probative if it:

(i) bears to have been signed by the granter of it;

(ii) is signed by a witness; and

(iii) the witness' name and address is stated. See *Obligationes literis*.

Procedure Roll.

See **Rolls**.

Process.

The name given to the collected writs, forms, interlocutors and pleadings from the first step down to final judgment, by which a civil action is brought in the Sheriff Court or Court of Session.

Process caption.

A summary warrant to imprison a person who has borrowed a process and is failing to return it.

Pro confesso.

"As confessed"; a person is usually held as confessed, i.e. as admitting the claim, when he does not appear to answer it.

Procuration.

Really agency or managership, but not used in this wide sense in Scots law; practically confined to agency to sign bills of exchange.

Procurator.

A general term for a person who acts for or instead of another under his authority; hence, sometimes applied to a solicitor appearing in court on behalf of a client.

Pro-curator.

See *Pro-tutor*.

Procurator fiscal.

Literally the procurator for the **fiscal** or **treasury**, he is an officer appointed by the Lord Advocate as his agent to act as public prosecutor within the jurisdiction of one of the six sheriffdoms of Scotland at sheriff and district court level. In addition the Procurator fiscal investigates and reports serious crimes to Crown Office, orders the investigation of sudden or suspicious deaths and has power to initiate fatal accident inquiries. The police act as the agents of the Procurator fiscal when investigating crime and report findings to him. See **Advocate, Lord**.

Procuratory.

A mandate or commission granted by one person to another.

Production.

A written document, produced as evidence in court. Where an item is not a written document it is normally referred to as a "Label".

Pro forma.

(i) As a mere formality.

(ii) A document used as a form or style.

Progress of titles.

The series of successive and linking recorded sasine title deeds, extending over at least 10 years, that, prior to registration under the Land Registration (Scotland) Act 1979, constitutes evidence of a secure title to heritable property.

Pro hac vice.

For this occasion.

Pro indiviso.

In an undivided state, usually in relation to property held by several persons. See **Common property**.

Pro loco et tempore.

For the place and time, used when a prosecutor deserts criminal proceedings while reserving the right to start anew. See **Desert**.

Promissory note.

An unconditional promise in writing to pay money.

Pro non scripto.

Words or phrases in a document to be disregarded or treated as if not included, e.g. illegal or impossible conditions in a will.

Proof.

The establishment of some fact by the bringing of evidence; also often used as an alternative to the word "evidence" itself. In addition to its general meaning, this word has the formal sense of the determination of a case by a judge alone (as opposed to jury trial). Where evidence is heard on the facts before questions of law are determined, there is said to be a *proof before answer*.

Propel.

Of an heir of entail, to anticipate the succession of his heir—apparent by giving him enjoyment of the entailed property before his succession in due course. The noun *propulsion* is also used.

Proper liferenter.

See **liferent**.

Propone.

To advance, put forward, propound.

Pro rata.

Proportionately.

Pro re nata.

As the occasion arises.

Prorogate.

(i) To *prorogate jurisdiction* means to waive objections to an otherwise incompetent jurisdiction.

(ii) To extend the time, as for e.g. (a) an arbitration, (b) a step in process or (c) the validity of a lease.

Pro tanto.

To that extent; for so much; to account of.

Protest, Notarial.

Demands for payment of money due in a bill of exchange may be made by way of a notarial instrument in which the notary "protests" that the debtor shall be liable on non-payment to suffer the consequences set forth in the instrument.

Protestation.

The procedure by which a defender in the Court of Session compels the pursuer who has not lodged the summons for calling either to proceed with his action or end it.

Protocol.

(i) A record of a diplomatic agreement or transaction.

(ii) A book used by a notary for recording acts done in the performance of his functions, e.g. **Protest**.

Pro-tutor; pro-curator.

Persons who act as tutors or curators without right.

Prout de jure.

A man who is entitled to prove his case *prout de jure* is entitled to use all means known to the law.

Pro veritate.

As if true. Often used in the course of a legal debate to indicate that for present purposes a particular written pleading or statement of a witness should be taken at its highest, i.e. assumed to be true.

Proving the tenor.

An action in which the pursuer seeks to set up a lost or destroyed document by proof of its contents (by reference to drafts, copies or parole evidence).

Provost.

The chief magistrate in a burgh as formerly constituted. He is styled *Lord Provost* in Edinburgh, Glasgow, Perth, Aberdeen, and Dundee.

Proximate cause.

In delict the effective factor actually causing the loss or harm as opposed to more remote factors which can be disregarded; hence the maxim "*causa proxima et non remota spectator*" (the near and not the remote cause is regarded).

Proxy.

A person appointed to act and vote for another, e.g. at a meeting of shareholders of a company; also applied to the document appointing such a person.

Public burdens.

A quasi-technical expression applied to taxes and the like as they affect land.

Public General Act.

A statute of general application as opposed to a **Private Act of Parliament**.

Punctum temporis.

Point of time.

Pupil.

Formerly girls up to 12 years and boys up to 14 years, the state of pupillarity being now abolished by the Age of Legal Capacity (Scotland) Act 1991. See **Minor; Nonage**.

Purge.

Used of an irritancy, it means to clear off the irritancy by payment or by remedying some failure that produced the irritancy. The noun is *purgation*.

Purify.

Fulfil or remove or discharge the condition attaching to a conditional obligation.

Pursuer.

The person suing in a civil action. The English equivalent is plaintiff.

Putative.

Believed, reputed or supposed; as applied, e.g.: (i) to a marriage considered valid; or (ii) to the alleged father of an illegitimate child.

Q

Qua.

In a certain character or capacity other than that of the individual concerned, e.g. as trustee.

Quadriennium utile.

The four years following on the attainment of majority, during which a minor could seek the reduction of his contracts if made to his *enorm lesion*. Abolished since 1991, the Age of Legal Capacity (Scotland) Act 1991 now provides instead for a young person's transaction to be set aside on the ground of prejudice (limited in time until attainment of age 21). See **Minor; Lesion**.

Quaere. (pr. "kwy-rye")

Indicates that a question is raised affecting some statement or proposition.

Qualify.

To make out or establish, as in the expression, *to qualify a title*.

Quam primum.

Forthwith or as soon as possible.

Quanti minoris.

The action, *quanti minoris* (literally, action of, or for, how much of less) is an action for the amount by which purported fulfilment of a contract of sale falls short of what was agreed.

Quantum.

Literally "how much". An amount fixed or specified in money as in a claim for damages. In any claim for damages there are always potentially two matters in issue: the liability of the defender and the quantification (value) of the claim. Either of the two issues may be agreed, while the other is not. For example, while a claim may be agreed between parties as being worth a particular sum of money, the defenders may nevertheless deny liability to pay that agreed sum.

Quantum lucratus.

Shortened form of "*In quantum lucratus est*", meaning "in so far as he has gained or profited". *Lucratus* refers only to pure gain or profit, unlike the principle embodied in the rule of *quantum meruit*. Often a person may have to account to another in law to the extent of the total amount by which he has gained. The phrase involves the idea of gain or profit apart from deserts, which distinguishes it from *quantum meruit*. See *Lucratus*; **Unjustified enrichment**.

Quantum meruit.

Literally, *tantum* being understood, "as much as he has earned"; an action *quantum meruit* may be pursued where work has been done for value but where the amount has not been fixed by contract. *Quantum meruit* arises from the implied obligation on an employer to pay a person performing work as much as he deserves, or can reasonably ask for his services. See *Quantum lucratus*; **Unjustified enrichment**.

Quantum valeat.

For what it is worth.

Quasi.

As if, as though.

Quasi-contract.

Quasi-contractual obligations are implied by the law and, unlike contract, do not arise because of consent between the two parties. The law of unjust enrichment provides examples. See **Contract; Delict; Unjustified enrichment**.

Quasi-delict.

Quasi-delictual actions are implied by the law; unlike delict, however, quasi-delictual obligations involve strict liability without the necessity of establishing *culpa*. See *Culpa*; **Delict**.

Queen's and Lord Treasurer's Remembrancer.

The general administrator of Crown revenues in Scotland responsible for the collection of certain fines and penalties, for auditing the account of sheriff clerks and procurators fiscal, administering treasure-trove and taking charge of the estates of persons falling to the Crown as *ultimus haeres*. In practice the office is held by the Crown Agent Designate at Crown Office.

Queen's Counsel.

A public appointment, based on merit, and conferred by the Crown on senior members of the Faculty of Advocates in Scotland (or barristers in England, Wales, Northern Ireland or elsewhere in the Commonwealth), distinguishing them as "senior counsel" through the initials "Q.C." after their surname. A Queen's Counsel is entitled to wear a black silk gown in court and is accordingly often referred to as a "silk". When the monarch is male, the title is "King's Counsel" and the initials are "K.C." The appointment is occasionally conferred honorarily upon professors and solicitors.

Quid iuris.

Meaning "what is the law?", it is a form of question often used in proposing a doubtful or difficult case.

Quid pro quo.

Something given in return for something else. For example, in the contract of sale, the price paid for the goods.

Quoad.

As regards.

Quoad ultra.

Literally, "as regards the above". A phrase much loved by litigators, it is invariably used in Defences in the form "*Quoad ultra* denied", meaning the averments of the pursuer, unless specifically admitted, are generally denied. See **Defences**.

Quorum.

The minimum number of persons necessary to constitute a meeting of a company or other body.

Quota.

A share or proportion.

R

Rack rent.

A term of English law, meaning the full or maximum rent obtainable for a heritable property.

Rank.

To be admitted as a claimant in one's rightful place, as in a bankruptcy; also, transitively, to admit as a claimant.

Rape.

The crime committed by a male when his penis enters a female's vagina without her consent. Proof that the female's will had been overcome (by force or otherwise) is no longer necessary to constitute the crime.

Ratio decidendi.

The rule or principle of law on which the decision of the court in a particular case is based. See **Obiter dictum**.

Real action.

An action, founded on a right of property in something, brought for the purpose of recovering that thing. A real action is referred to in Roman law as *vindicatio*. See *Condictio*.

Real burden.

In the law of conveyance of heritable property, an obligation that is laid upon lands and not on a person and that, in order to be effective, must enter the property register. When it secures the right to a sum of money it is termed a pecuniary real burden. In other cases a more appropriate term is real condition.

Real raiser.

See **Multiplepoinding**.

Real right.

A right available against the world in general (*jus in re*) as, for instance, a right of property. See *Jus in rem*.

Real warrandice.

See **Warrandice**.

Rebus integris.

Matters being complete. Where an agreement has been entered into with reference to a contract but nothing done in dependence upon it by the parties, matters are said to be "complete", so that either of them can resile. If, however, actings have followed upon the agreement, the parties are barred from resiling, because *res non est integra* (literally, "the matter is no longer complete"). See *Rei interventus*; **Personal bar**.

Rebut.

To lead evidence or arguments countering the testimony or assertions of the other party to a dispute or litigation.

Receiver.

An insolvency practitioner, appointed by the holder of a **floating charge** (or by the Court of Session, on application to it), in order to manage and control a limited company in the place of its directors. The receiver must manage and control the limited company in the interests of the holder of the floating charge, the other creditors and the company itself. Floating charges are most commonly held by banks; and receivers are consequently most often appointed when the limited company defaults on its bank loans. The term has a wider application in England where an official receiver functions in matters such as bankruptcy.

Reclaim.

To reclaim is to appeal against a decision of a Court of Session Outer House or vacation judge. The appeal is to the **Inner House**. Reclaiming is by a *reclaiming motion*, formerly by *reclaiming note*.

Recompense.

See **Unjustified enrichment**.

Reconvention.

A right in A to counterclaim or cross-claim against X (who is in another jurisdiction) in A's jurisdiction. The claim is allowed where X has already brought an action against A in A's jurisdiction.

Record.

The statements of their respective claims and answers by parties to an action, lodged in court; when finally adjusted it is *closed* by order of the court and becomes the *closed record:* up to then it is the *open record.* When used in this sense the word bears the accent on the second syllable.

Records.

A general expression used in referring to the property registers, or the filing departments of the court, and meaning that one that is appropriate to the document under consideration. A deed is said to *enter the records* when it is registered or recorded. So too "the register" is used in a general sense.

Recourse.

As a legal term, means the right that a person as the assignee of a right may have, when the right fails, to go after the assignor of the right for relief.

Reddendo. (pr. "re-den-dow")

In feudal law, the duty or service to be paid or rendered by vassal to superior as provided by a feu-charter: from the words of the clause, *reddendo inde annuatim.* The word is also used as the name of the clause.

Redeemable.

Meaning subject to a right of redemption (by the debtor), it describes the right of a security holder as contrasted with the absolute or irredeemable right of a proprietor.

Reduce.

To annul or set aside by legal process; hence *reduction* (the action to set aside a deed) and *reduction-improbation*, which is the name given to a reduction when forgery is the ground on which it is sought; *reduction-reductive* is the reducing of a decree of reduction that has been improperly obtained.

Redundancy.

The position of an employee dismissed because his job has ceased to exist entitling him by statute to a redundancy payment.

Re-engagement order.

An employment tribunal order for reinstatement in comparable or other suitable employment of an employee unfairly dismissed.

Re-examination.

The examination of a witness in court by or for the party calling him, following upon his cross-examination by or for the opposing party.

Regalia.

Crown rights, some of which, the *regalia majora* as, e.g. the right to hold the **seashore** in trust for the public, are inalienable, whilst others, the *regalia minora* as, e.g. the right of salmon-fishing, can be the subject of a grant.

Regiam Majestatem.

"The Auld Lawes and Constitutions of Scotland", it is the name (derived from the first two words of the treatise) of an early manual of laws and practice dating from the fourteenth century and the reign of King David I of Scotland. It was first printed in 1609 as edited by Sir John Skene.

Region.

One of the nine areas into which Scotland is divided for local government purposes, each of which is divided into districts.

Registration for execution.

The registration in the Books of Council and Session (i.e. of the Court of Session) or books of a sheriff court of a deed constituting an obligation and embodying the obligant's consent to its registration. Such registration has the effect of a decree of court for the purpose of enforcement. Often combined with registration for preservation.

Registration for preservation.

The registration of any deed in the Books of Council and Session or the books of a sheriff court to obviate the risk of loss, making copies or extracts equivalent to the original obtainable. Often combined with registration for execution.

Registration for publication.

The registration or recording of deeds relating to land in the General Register of Sasines making public their content and giving the grantee a real right to the interest created with priority in accordance with the date of registration.

Registration of title.

The system of registration of interests in land now being introduced progressively in Scotland to replace registration of deeds as operative under registration for publication. Under this system, the title to an interest rests on the entry in the register without reference to any deeds and is guaranteed by the state.

Rei interitus.

The destruction of a thing or its ceasing to exist. *Rei interitus* renders a contract concerning it unenforceable or impossible of performance.

Rei interventus.

When A in full knowledge permits X, who has contracted with him, to do something on the faith of the contract, obligation or trust, which is lacking in form and so open to challenge, that is *rei interventus* and it bars A from challenging the contract. The rule of *rei interventus* has since 1995 been replaced by statute. For the replacement rule, see **Homologation**.

Relevant.

The pertinence of evidence to a fact in issue in litigation is a matter of relevance. Relevance is often described as the most fundamental requirement of any evidence, since irrelevant evidence is always inadmissible. A legal claim or charge in whatever form, is said to be relevant when it can be said that were the facts alleged proved, the remedy sought would be granted. The noun is *relevancy*. A *plea to relevancy* is an attack upon the relevancy.

Relict.

A widow or widower. See ***Jus relictae*; *Jus relicti*.**

Relocation.

Re-letting. See **Tacit relocation**.

Remand.

The remittal of a person in custody or on bail upon the adjournment of criminal proceedings. Hence, "remand prisoners" are those held in custody awaiting trial.

Remissio injuriae.

Forgiveness of an offence or the condoning of it. The classic example is from an action for divorce founded on adultery, where there is a defence based on the defendant having been forgiven by the pursuer for the adulterous act.

Remit.

The transfer of some matter by one judge to another, but more often by a judge to a person named by him as, e.g. to an expert "man of skill" (such as an accountant) in order that the latter may inquire and report.

Removing.

A removing, or an action of removing, is one by which the landlord rids himself of a tenant whose term has expired or who has incurred an irritancy. The former is an *ordinary*, the latter is an *extraordinary* removing. See **Ejection**.

Rent.

The return, which may be in produce or corporeal moveables but is now nearly always in money, given by a tenant or hirer for the use of property or goods subject to lease or hire.

Rentaller.

See **Kindly tenant**.

Renvoi.

The "catch-22" problem arising in international private law when the rules of one system refer the decision of a point of law to another system, the rules of which refer the matter back to the first system. See **Foreign jurisdiction**.

Reparation.

The making good of a civil wrong, usually by an award of damages.

Repeal.

Revocation or cancellation applied particularly to the cancellation of statutory provisions by subsequent legislation.

Repel.

A Scottish court does not overrule a plea or an objection, it *repels* it.

Repetition.

See **Unjustified enrichment**.

Replication, Proof in.

Evidence allowed to be given by a pursuer after the defender has concluded his proof, where something has come out that could not have been anticipated.

Repone.

To repone a defender is to restore him to his position as a litigant when decree in absence has been given against him. Also competent in, e.g. case of failure to lodge documents in appeal to Court of Session.

Reporter.

A person appointed to hold a public inquiry; also applied to professional persons, lawyers or others, to whom the court may remit some aspect of a case for investigation or advice; to the officers responsible for bringing cases before Children's Hearings Panels; and also to those who prepare and compile the published reports of cases decided by the courts.

Representation.

(i) A person is said to represent another when he stands in place of that other, his predecessor, in a matter of succession.

(ii) The entitlement of a person to have his case before a court or tribunal presented by someone such as a lawyer acting on his behalf.

(iii) In the law of succession the right of issue of a beneficiary predeceasing the date of vesting to take the beneficiary's share.

(iv) A statement made by a person to influence another to enter into a contract with that person.

Reprobate.

See **Approbate**.

Requisition.

A demand by a creditor for repayment of a debt, sometimes through the agency of a notary.

Resale price maintenance.

Restriction or control of the price at which a purchaser may resell goods he has bought.

Rescission.

The cancellation or termination by one party of a contract alleged to have been wrongfully induced or materially breached by the other party.

Res communes.

Things in their nature incapable of appropriation such as light and air.

Resealing.

The process formerly but no longer necessary to render Scottish confirmation of executors effective in England or English probate or letters of administration effective in Scotland.

Reservation.

A provision in a deed whereby the grantor reserves some right or rights for himself.

Reserved matters.

Under the devolution settlement, the areas of legislative and governmental competence retained by the UK government and parliament and therefore outwith the control of the **Scottish Parliament**. Reserved matters include the UK Constitution, registration and funding of political parties, foreign affairs, the civil service, defence and treason. Control of all matters not reserved are devolved. See **Devolved matters**.

Reset (or reset of theft).

The crime of receiving stolen property, knowing it to have been stolen.

Res furtivae.

Things stolen and hence tainted, so that property in them remains in the original owner despite subsequent honest dealings.

Res gestae.

Literally the things done; the circumstances. Statements that form part of the circumstances attendant upon an act may often be admissible evidence despite the rule excluding **hearsay evidence**.

Residue.
What remains of a testator's estate after debts, expenses and specific or pecuniary legacies have been met, the person or persons sharing the remainder being termed residuary legatees.

Resignation.
The giving up of some office or appointment, e.g. by a trustee or a company director.

Resignation, Instrument of.
See under **Instrument of resignation**.

Res inter alios acta.
A transaction between parties A and X is usually irrelevant to a question between A and B: it is *res inter alios acta*, "something which took place among others".

Res ipsa loquitur.
The thing speaks for itself; as where the fact of accident is in the circumstances sufficient to infer fault and civil liability.

Res judicata.
A question decided by competent legal proceedings, which cannot again be raised.

Res merae facultatis.
A right is *res merae facultatis* when, being exercisable or not at pleasure, it cannot be lost by prescription. Examples include the right of a proprietor to build upon his own property or the right to sail upon the sea.

Res mercatoria.
Commerce: a document in *re mercatoria* may be accepted as valid, though not formal, in order to facilitate commerce.

Res noviter veniens ad notitiam.
Information newly discovered, sometimes justifying the admission of new matter in a case, or a new trial.

Res nullius.
A thing, in the widest sense, that never had an owner, or that had but has now lost its owner.

Resolution.
The decision of a meeting on some matter submitted to its consideration.

Resolutive.
Of a condition; one that brings a right or obligation to an end if a specified event occurs. See **Irritancy; Suspensive**.

Res perit suo domino.
The owner for the time being of any property bears the risk of its accidental destruction. Thus, when a subject is hired out, any

deterioration it may suffer, or its total loss, falls upon the owner and not upon the hirer, so long as the hirer uses it for the purposes for which it was hired.

Respondent.

The successful party in a civil action defending on appeal the decision of the lower court in his favour.

Res publicae.

Things in which the property resides in the state alone, like navigable rivers and highways.

Resting-owing.

An expression used both as adjective and noun. As the former it simply means, of a debt, unpaid. The resting-owing of a debt is its state of not having been paid.

Restitutio in integrum.

The restoration of a person to the same position as he would have occupied had he never entered into some transaction.

Restitution.

See **Unjustified enrichment**.

Resumption.

The re-possession by the landlord of part of the subjects let in terms of a power to that effect in the lease.

Res universitatis.

Things belonging to a corporation whose use is common to the members.

Retention.

The withholding by one party to a contract of due performance in order to compel the other party to give due performance. It is particularly used with reference to the retention of moveable property until a debt due by its owner is paid. See **Lien**.

Retentis.

See ***In retentis***.

Re-trial.

See **New trial**.

Retro.

Backwards, referring to an act or occurrence having retrospective effect.

Retrocession.

Re-conveyance of a right to him who gave it.

Return, Clause of.

See **Clause**.

Reversion.

A right of redemption, e.g. of subjects conveyed in security of a debt: sometimes applied more widely as in England to the interest of an owner while subject to some temporary interest such as a **liferent** or a tenancy.

Review.

Revision and reconsideration of a judicial decision by a higher court on appeal.

Rider (or **riding claim** or **interest**).

A liquid claim upon a claimant in a **multiplepoinding** that may be lodged in the multiplepoinding itself.

Riever. (pr. "ree-ver")

Robber: perhaps especially the freebooter who lived on blackmail.

Right of way.

The right of a person either as an individual in the case of a servitude right or as a member of the public in the case of a public right of way to traverse a specified or recognised route over the property of another person.

Rioting.

See **Mobbing and rioting**.

Risk.

The possibility of loss or damage as covered by an insurance policy. See also *Res perit suo domino*.

Rolls.

The official lists of cases and court business as set down for hearing. In the Court of Session, the rolls of court are set by the Keeper of the Rolls. They are split into the General Roll and the Daily Roll. In the **Outer House** of the Court of Session the Daily Roll consists of *the calling list; motion roll;, diet roll; procedure roll; commercial roll; adjustment roll; by order (adjustment) roll; by order roll; proof and jury trial roll; judgement roll* and *undefended divorce roll*. In the **Inner House**, the Daily Roll consists of the *single bills; by order roll; summar roll* and *advisings*.

Roup. (pr. "rowp")

Auction. **Articles of roup** are the conditions in terms of which property is exposed to sale by auction.

Royal Assent.

The approval by the sovereign of a Bill passed by Parliament whereby the Bill becomes an Act.

Rubric.

Of a statute, the title at one time printed in red; of a reported decision, the head-note.

Rules of Court.

Rules setting out the procedure to be followed in civil and criminal actions. Civil actions in the Court of Session are governed by the Rules of the Court of Session; civil actions in the sheriff court by the Ordinary and Summary Cause Rules. The rules are formulated under statutory powers in the form of **Acts of Sederunt** by the Lords of Council and Session with the advice of Rules Councils. In criminal actions the rules for the High Court of Justiciary are set out by **Acts of Adjournal** and in the Sheriff Court by Statute.

Runrig or **runridge lands.**

A plan of land ownership in which alternate ridges of a field belong to different people.

S

Salvage.

A reward payable by maritime law or under contract for saving or preserving an endangered vessel or its cargo: the principle now applies also to aircraft.

Sasine.

A seising or putting into possession of land to confer a real right, originally done by handing over of earth or stone, later by registration of an instrument of sasine, and now by registration of the conveyance itself or if, being in general terms, it is unsuitable for registration, the registration of a notice of title (formerly a notarial instrument). See **Registration for publication**.

Scienter. (pr. "ski-enter")

This word is sometimes used, in defiance of grammar, to designate the knowledge possessed by the owner of an animal that the animal is savage.

Scotland Office.

Following devolution, the office of government at Westminster presided over by the Secretary of State for Scotland. The function of the Scotland Office was to represent Scottish interests within the UK government in matters reserved to Westminster in terms of the devolved settlement. The office of **Advocate General for Scotland** formed part of the Scotland Office. Following June 2003 the Scotland Office now forms part of the Department for Constitutional Affairs. See **Scottish Executive; Advocate General for Scotland**.

Scottish Acts of Parliament.

Acts of the old Scottish Parliament prior to the Treaty of Union in 1707, as distinct from **Acts of the Scottish Parliament** which are devolved legislation passed by the new parliament since 1999.

Scottish Administration.

Employees of the UK Home Civil Service appointed by Ministers of the **Scottish Executive** to assist with the governance of Scotland's devolved matters.

Scottish Executive.

The government of Scotland, devolved from Westminster. It is responsible for devolved matters including health, education, justice, rural affairs and transport. *Reserved matters* remain in the control of the UK government. Prior to devolution, much of the work of the Scottish Executive was carried out by the Scottish Office. See **Reserved matters; Devolved matters**.

Scottish Land Court.

A court established by statute with a legally qualified chairman having judicial status and members with agricultural expertise. Its jurisdiction covers the various forms of agricultural tenancy, crofts, smallholdings and agricultural holdings. The jurisdiction of the Land Court has been extended by the Agricultural Holdings (Scotland) Act 2002 to incorporate the functions previously carried out by the process of Agricultural Arbitration. The Court operates at two levels:

(i) a Divisional Court where applications are heard by a Court member and a legal assessor; or

(ii) as a Full Court with a **quorum** of two members and the Chairman. The Court's decision is issued as an Order and is binding on the parties concerned. There is a right of appeal to the Court of Session but only on questions of law. The Chairman of the Scottish Land Court has the same rank and tenure of office as a judge in the Court of Session.

Scottish Law Commission.

A government body established to promote in Scotland proposals for law reform and for the modernisation and simplification of existing laws. The Law Commission performs similar functions in respect of English law.

Scottish Office.

Prior to devolution, the name commonly used to describe collectively the departments of government under the control of the Secretary of State for Scotland performing the functions for which he was responsible under statute, common law or custom. The functions of the Scottish Office have largely been passed to the **Scottish Executive**. See **Scotland Office**.

Scottish Parliament.

A legislative body created by a statute of the United Kingdom parliament at Westminster and granted the power to legislate in the area of Scottish **devolved matters**. It is comprised of a single debating chamber and a system of committees with power to propose and scrutinize legislation. It has members elected on a proportional representation basis as well as by means of the Westminster constituency system.

Scottish Parliamentary Corporate Body.

Also known as the **Parliamentary Corporation**, it is a statutory corporate body created to provide property, staff and services to the Scottish Parliament and has power to enter into legal obligations in order to do so. The Corporation is comprised of the **Presiding Officer** and four members of the **Scottish Parliament**.

Scottish Public Services Ombudsman.

The **ombudsman** for **devolved matters**. The office is an amalgamation of the various ombudsmen and complaints processes for the Scottish Parliament, the Scottish Health Service, local government, the Housing Association, Scottish Enterprise, Highlands & Islands Enterprise and the Mental Welfare Commission.

Seal.

A stamped symbol impressed on documents to symbolise authenticity. It is used primarily by corporate bodies, companies and notaries public. The Scottish Seal (kept by the **First Minister**) is the seal appointed by the Treaty of Union to be used in place of the Great Seal of Scotland.

Search for encumbrances (or **incumbrances**).

The process of inspection of the registers, in order to ascertain the validity of a title to land and whether or not any deeds or diligences prejudicial to the title exist.

Search warrant.

A warrant granted by a magistrate or sheriff to search for goods or documents that might form evidence in criminal proceedings.

Seashore (or **foreshore**).

The land between the high water and low water marks of ordinary tides vested in the Crown, or someone having a Crown grant but subject always to certain public rights of way.

Secondary creditor.

One who holds a security that is postponed to another or others. See **Catholic creditor**.

Secured creditor.

A creditor holding a security for his debt.

Secure tenancy.

Defined by statute as "Scottish secure tenancies" it is a domestic tenancy granted by a local authority or other body with statutory powers for the provision of housing, giving the tenant protection in the form of security of tenure beyond the duration of any lease or tenancy contract. The corresponding arrangements in respect of private property are Regulated Tenancies if granted not later than January 2, 1989 and Assured Tenancies if granted after that date.

Security.

The element of fortification of an obligation, e.g. to pay money, represented by a guarantee or cautionary obligation, i.e. a *personal security*, as contrasted with a *real security* such as a pledge or conveyance of some item of the debtor's property as in the case of a heritable security over land. The term "securities" is also applied loosely to investments such as shares, loan stocks of companies or bond issues made by the government.

Sederunt.

Meaning "they sat". It can refer to:

(i) the attendance list usually incorporated in the minutes of a meeting; or

(ii) the records of proceedings in a sequestration kept by the permanent trustee are termed sederunt books. The same term is sometimes applied to records kept in connection with testamentary or other trusts.

Semble.

Literally "seemingly" introducing a statement or proposition about which there may be some doubt.

Senator of the College of Justice.

A judge of the Court of Session. An Act of 1540 so styles the judges.

Separatim.

Commonly used in civil pleadings, meaning, "separately" or "apart from anything else averred or argued".

Separation.

The judicial separation *a mensa et thoro* (i.e. at bed and board) of spouses who remain married.

Sequestration.

The act of rendering an individual bankrupt. Strictly, it is a man's estate that is sequestrated or set aside for the use of his creditors. To *sequestrate for rent* is to take a tenant's furniture, etc. to satisfy a claim for rent. Sequestration therefore means a process of bankruptcy, except where qualified by the words "for rent".

Seriatim. (pr. "serry-atim")

One after another.

Service; serve.

(i) Formal delivery of process, a judicial writ or other formal document to another person timeously and in the manner prescribed by law.

(ii) The duty owed by an employee to his employer in terms of a contract of employment for provision of his service (*locatio operarum*), e.g. as a domestic servant, as distinct from a specific contract for provision of particular services (*locatio operis faciendi*), e.g. to build a house. See **Location**.

(iii) An obsolete judicial proceeding that transmitted the ownership of land from a deceased person to his heir or established in a man his title of heir to the deceased.

Servient tenement.

See **Servitude**.

Servitude.

A burden over a piece of land, the **servient tenement**, in favour of a neighbouring piece of land, the **dominant tenement**, whereby the servient tenement is either;

(i) restrained from the full use of what is the servient tenement's own (a **negative servitude**); or

(ii) obliged to allow the **dominant tenement** to do something upon the servient tenement *(a positive servitude)*. The servitude is created by express or implied agreement. *Legal servitudes* are imposed by law: *conventional servitudes* by agreement of parties. *Praedial servitudes* are servitudes over land: the single *personal servitude* is the **liferent**. Servitudes are also categorised as *urban* or *rural*. The urban servitudes are:

(i) **support** (subdivided into *Tigni immittendi* and *Oneris ferendi*);

(ii) **stillicide**; and

(iii) **light and prospect** (subdivided into *Non aedificandi*, *Altius non tollendi* and *Non officiendi luminibus*).

The rural servitudes are:

(i) *iter*, or way;

(ii) *aquaehaustus*;

(iii) *aquaeductus*;

(iv) **pasturage**; and

(v) **fuel, feal and divot**. See passim for specific definitions and also **Wayleave**.

Session, Court of.

The supreme civil court in Scotland, with both original (**Outer House**) and appellate (**Inner House**) jurisdiction. An appeal presently lies to the House of Lords in London.

Sessions.

The periods in the year as fixed annually and separated by vacations during which periods the Court of Session and the sheriff courts deal with civil cases.

Set; sett.

An old-fashioned word meaning, to let. Also as a noun: (i) a lease; (ii) the constitution of a burgh as formerly existing.

Set-off (or compensation).

A debtor's right to have a money debt reduced or extinguished in respect of his having a similar claim against the creditor.

Sett and sale, Action of.
    An action by X, a part owner of a ship, claiming that the others buy X's share, or sell their own, or that the ship be sold.

Settlement.
    (i) The disposal of property by will or other deed constituting a trust.
    (ii) An agreement or compromise concluding a dispute or litigation.
    (iii) The completion of a heritable property transaction.

Shareholder.
    In company law, a holder of the stock of a company, usually divided into shares and represented by transferable share certificates. The shareholders individually have a separate legal persona from the company, and by virtue of the principle of "limited liability", shareholders are each only liable to the company to the extent of their capital contribution (usually in the form of purchase of shares). Shareholders have voting rights in relation to the running of the company and can be entitled to receive annual distribution of the company's profits in proportion to their respective shareholdings. See **Limited liability**.

Sheriff.
    The holder of an ancient judicial and administrative office, once hereditary, when the effective officer was the *sheriff-depute*, now obsolete. Today we have the *sheriff-principal* mainly hearing civil appeals from sheriffs (formerly called *sheriffs-substitute*) who are judges with all but unlimited civil jurisdiction and important criminal jurisdiction. *Honorary sheriffs* who may or may not be legally qualified persons are appointed for convenience to relieve the sheriff, on occasion, of his less important duties, and qualified persons may be appointed as *part-time sheriffs*.

Sheriff-clerk.
    The principal clerk of the court in a **sheriffdom**, now a civil servant.

Sheriff-court.
    The court of the sheriff in which crime is tried summarily and on indictment (three years' imprisonment being the maximum penalty), and civil cases of unlimited value, with a few exceptions, may be heard.

Sheriffdom.
    The area in which a sheriff-principal exercises jurisdiction. There are six such areas in Scotland each divided into sheriff court districts.

Sheriff-officer.
    A person by whom process is served and diligence carried out in sheriff court proceedings. See **Messengers-at-Arms**.

Shewers. (pr. "shoo-ers")
    Persons named by the court to accompany and show to the jurors the premises or other object to which a dispute relates, when a view is allowed.

Signet, The Queen's.

The Seal of the Court of Session with which are sealed "whatever passes by the warrant of the Session". These were formerly signed exclusively by "Writers to the Signet", a body of solicitors that to this day forms a society apart. See **Keeper of the Signet**.

Sine die. (pr. "sin-ey dee-ey")

As of a continuation, without fixed date, indefinitely.

Sine qua non.

An essential condition or factor without which nothing can be done: a person may be appointed a sine qua non trustee.

Single bills.

See **Rolls**.

Singular successor.

A purchaser or acquirer of property obtaining it otherwise than by succession on the death of the owner (e.g. a purchaser, creditor or donee). See **Universal successor**.

Singuli in solidum.

See **Joint and several**.

Si petitur tantum.

Meaning "only if asked [for]". It is applied to such items as "peppercorn" rents or feuduties of nominal amount.

Si sine liberis decesserit.

"If he shall have died without children"; these words express the content of two implied conditions in the law of succession:

(i) the *conditio si testator sine liberis decesserit*, which means that a person's will, if it does not deal with children, is presumed to be revoked by the subsequent birth of a child; and

(ii) the *conditio si institutus sine liberis decesserit*, which means that in case of a bequest to descendants or nephews and nieces, their issue, though not mentioned, may take, if the descendants or nephews and neices themselves have predeceased.

Sist.

(i) To stay or stop process.

(ii) To summon or call as a party.

Skat duty.

See **Udal tenure**.

Slander.

See **Defamation**.

Small claims procedure.

The informal procedure in the sheriff court now applying to claims not exceeding £750 in monetary value.

Small debt jurisdiction.

The jurisdiction of the sheriff as formerly exercised in the sheriff small debt court in actions involving £50 or under; now abolished, such cases being dealt with by the **Small claims procedure**.

Small holding.

An agricultural tenancy of limited size located outwith the crofting counties and regulated by the Small Landholders (Scotland) Acts: the basis of tenure being similar to that of a **croft**.

Socius criminis.

Accomplice in a crime.

Solatium.

Damages given by way of reparation for injury to feelings.

Solemn procedure.

The procedure under which a person charged on indictment is tried by a sheriff or judge of the High Court of Justiciary with a jury of 15, the votes of eight being sufficient for a conviction.

Solicitor.

The generic term for persons engaged in legal practice otherwise than as members of the Bar including those sometimes designated law agents, writers or procurators. A *solicitor-advocate* is a solicitor granted rights of audience before the Court of Session, High Court of Justiciary and other superior courts. Solicitor-advocates, like solicitors, are regulated by the **Law Society of Scotland**.

Solicitors before the Supreme Courts ("S.S.C.").

A body of solicitors practising in Edinburgh that was incorporated in 1797.

Solicitor General.

One of the two Scottish law officers, the other being the **Lord Advocate**. Following devolution, the Solicitor General is a member of the **Scottish Executive** appointed by The Queen on the recommendation of the **First Minister**, together with the agreement of the **Scottish Parliament** (of which the Solicitor General can, but need not, be a member). He is the Lord Advocate's assistant legal adviser to the Scottish Executive.

Solum.

The bed of a watercourse or the ground on which buildings have been erected.

Sowming and rowming, Action of.

An action formerly in use in which it was determined how many cattle the parties entitled to a common grazing area might each pasture thereon. Such questions as arising in crofting communities are dealt with by the **Scottish Land Court**.

Special case.
A convenient mode of obtaining the opinion of the **Inner House** of the Court of Session on a point of law where the facts are not in dispute. The term is also applied to appeals from the **Scottish Land Court** to the Court of Session although they are really a kind of stated case.

Special defence.
A defence to a criminal charge which must be intimated before the trial, e.g. alibi or self-defence.

Special destination.
A special destination effects some departure from the legally implied line of succession as respects a particular property.

Special verdict.
A verdict of a civil jury not finding "aye" or "no" as to the issue or issues but making certain findings in fact, to which the Court later applies the law.

Specificatio.
Deriving from Roman law, it is a mode of acquiring property by making a new object, *species*, out of material belonging to another.

Specific implement.
The actual performance of a contractual obligation not being one for the payment of money; See *Ad factum praestandum*.

Spei emptio.
The purchase of a chance as, e.g. of a succession.

Spes successionis.
An expectancy of succession as distinguished from a vested right. Such expectation has a value and may be used for security.

Sponsio ludicra (pl. sponsiones ludicrae).
An agreement made in sport as, e.g. a wager, and unenforceable in any court proceedings.

Spuilzie. (pr. "spoolie")
The taking away of moveables from another's possession against his will forming a ground of civil action under that name.

Squatter.
A person occupying premises without having right or title to do so.

Stamp duty.
A tax payable on certain legal documents with payment as evidenced by an impressed or affixed stamp being required for the effectiveness or enforceability of the document and for its entry in a public register.

Standard charge.
The real burden affecting heritable properties in respect of the amount of minister's stipend as standardised and allocated under statutory provisions.

Standard security.
The form of statutory heritable security that is used to create a security over an interest in land. The relevant statutory provisions include certain Standard Conditions variable only within limits prescribed.

Stare decisis. (pr. 'starry – dekeesis')
Adherence to precedent, i.e. the principle that court decisions will be bound by the earlier decisions of superior courts.

Stated case.
A form of procedure or appeal whereby a court such as the Court of Session is required to determine the law applicable to facts as found by a tribunal or lower court or to circumstances arising in proceedings pending before such tribunal or court. See **Special case.**

Status quo (ante).
The existing or present situation or state of affairs, status quo ante referring to the state of affairs existing before some date or event.

Statute.
An Act of the Westminster or **Scottish Parliament**, public or private.

Statutory Instrument ("SI").
The form in which orders, rules and regulations or other subordinate legislation are now made superseding, since 1947, statutory rules and orders (SR & O.). Statutory Instruments of the **Scottish Parliament** are referred to as SSI's.

Steelbow.
A custom by which a landlord delivered grain, cattle, tools, and the like to the tenant on the understanding that similar commodities should be given him at the end of the lease. Seemingly from *bow* meaning stock of a farm and *steel* in the metaphorical sense of rigidly fixed, i.e., in amount.

Stellionate.
(i) A crime that has no particular name.
(ii) In particular, all crimes involving fraud and having no special name. From Latin *stellionatus*, meaning knavery, cozenage.

Stillicide.
A servitude binding the holder of the servient tenement to receive water falling from the eaves of an adjoining house. Also referred to as **eavesdrop.**

Stipend.
The remuneration of a parish minister that,prior to becoming standard charge was based upon the teinds.

Stipendary magistrate.
A salaried person, legally qualified, appointed by a local authority as judge in a district court (particularly in Glasgow). See **Justice of the Peace; District Court.**

Stirpes, Succession *Per*.
See *Per stirpes*.

Stoppage *in transitu*.
The stopping and recall of goods sent by a seller, on his learning of the buyer's insolvency.

Strict liability.
Liability for loss or damage caused irrespective of fault.

***Stricti juris*.**
Strictly in accordance with the relevant legal rules.

Stouthrief. (pr. "stow (as in "how")-threef")
Theft by housebreaking or housebreaking with intent to steal.

Style.
(i) The name or title of a person.
(ii) A model form of deed or other document. Cf. Precedent in England.

Subinfeudation.
The granting of a feu by an owner of land other than the Crown, i.e. by an owner who himself holds on feudal tenure.

Subjects.
A word commonly used to mean property and usually heritable property. The singular, "subject," is occasionally used.

Sub judice.
In the hands of the law, as when the decision of a court or tribunal on some dispute before it is awaited.

Submission.
A deed by which parties agree to submit a disputed point to arbitration.

Subordinate legislation.
Rules or regulations, etc. made not by Parliament but under Parliament's authority and promulgated in statutory instruments. See **Statutory Instrument**.

Subornation of perjury.
The crime involved in inducing another person to commit perjury.

Subrogation.
The rule whereby a person discharging the liability of another acquires any right of relief or otherwise belonging to that other. The principle is especially significant in the law of insurance. An example arises where, following a collision between two cars, an injured party is compensated by his own insurer for the damage caused by the driver of the other car. The insurer is then subrogated into the insured person's claim against the other driver and may raise an action against him.

Substitute.
A person named in a destination of property to take on failure of the institute. See **Institute**.

Succession.

(i) Is universal when it involves the passing of property from one person to another on the death of the former with all attaching rights and liabilities (see *Per stirpes*; **Per capita**).

(ii) Is singular when particular items of property are transferred by sale or gift.

Sue.

To raise a civil action.

Sui juris.

Denotes persons of full legal capacity, i.e. not subject to the control of others as regards their legal acts. Those who are not sui juris include the insane and children under 16 years.

Summary.

In criminal matters, the term refers to proceedings on **complaint** instigated by the Procurator fiscal (as opposed to on **indictment**), and prosecuted before:

(i) a sheriff in the Sheriff Court; or

(ii) a Justice of the Peace or Stipendiary Magistrate in the District Court (as opposed to before a Jury in the Sheriff Court or High Court).

In civil proceedings in the sheriff court, the summary cause is the form of simplified procedure now applicable to a fairly wide category of cases, other than those dealt with under **Small claims procedure**, with a limit of £1,500 in the case of pecuniary claims. *Summary application* is a comprehensive name for applications that can be disposed of in a summary manner. *Summary diligence* refers to diligence proceeding on a deed or document registered for execution or on certain bills of exchange, in each case without an action constituting the debt. A *summary warrant* is a warrant issued by the sheriff to a local authority authorising diligence for the recovery of arrears of rates or Community Charge.

Summary trial.

(i) In civil cases the trial of a dispute or question by a judge in the **Outer House** of the Court of Session by consent of the parties on application initiated by summary petition, the trial taking place in court or in chambers by a simplified procedure.

(ii) In criminal cases the trial of an accused person by a sheriff, justice of the peace or magistrate without a jury.

Summons.

Most importantly, the usual form of writ in the Court of Session issued in name of the sovereign, signeted and containing a royal mandate to **messengers-at-arms** to cite the defender to the Court of Session. See **The Queen's Signet; Petition**.

Superior.

In feudal law, a person who makes a grant of land to another to "hold of" him as a **vassal**, in return for a perpetual payment of feuduty. His estate is one of *superiority*, also called the *dominium directum*.

Supersede.

Means in Scots law rather to postpone than to displace, as in the expression, *supersede extract.*

Supplementary summons.

Such a summons was formerly necessary in order to add parties or change the grounds of action in a case. Now the power of the Court to amend renders this unnecessary.

Support.

The servitude right of an owner of a building to have it supported. Alternatively, the right to let a beam or other structural part of the dominant building into the wall of the servient building and to keep it there. These two forms of the servitude are derived from the Civil law servitudes of *oneris ferendi* and *tigni immittendi* respectively.

Surrogate, (also *surrogatum*).

A substitute for something, as, for example, the price of land instead of the land.

Survivorship, Clause of.

(i) A provision in a will or the like by which the maker, taking into account the possibility that some of the persons to be benefited may die before taking the benefit, directs that their interests will pass to the survivors.

(ii) A conveyance of property to two or more persons and the survivor or survivors of them.

Suspend; suspension.

In civil matters, a process whereby diligence may be stayed and also a decree in absence or a decree of a lower court brought under review. *Suspension and interdict* is the process used to stay execution when simple suspension is no longer competent, and also, generally, to prevent injury to any right. In criminal matters, suspension is the setting aside of an improper warrant or a defective decision of a summary court raised by Bill of Suspension in the Court of Criminal Appeal. *Suspension and liberation* is used where the suspender is in prison.

Suspensive condition.

A condition that suspends the coming into force of a right or obligation until the condition is fulfilled; sometimes called a condition precedent, being the English term. See **Resolutive**.

T

Table, To.

In any ordinary action in the sheriff court that is being defended the pursuer or his solicitor must table (i.e. present) the writ or summons in court at the first calling of the case.

Tacit relocation.

Implied re-letting; the legal principle that where no notice is given to terminate a lease, the lease is renewed for a year (if originally for a year or more): and for the period of the lease if originally for less than a year. The principle extends to contracts of service and to partnerships.

Taciturnity.

Keeping silence about a debt when a claim would have been natural, leading to an inference of payment.

Tack.

A lease. The term is practically obsolete. The term **assedation** is also used.

Tailzie, tailye. (pr. as in "daily")

An old name for entail; a destination of heritage to a prescribed line of heirs, guarded by prohibitions and forfeiture, and only "breakable" on fulfilment of statutory conditions. New creations have been incompetent since 1914. Tailzie is also a verb—to **entail**. The "z" is mute.

Tantum et tale. (pr. "ta-lay")

So much and of such a kind, as applied, e.g. to property sold to and accepted by the purchaser with such advantages and disadvantages as it may have.

Taxation.

As applied to legal expenses or charges (including solicitors' or advocates' fees incurred in court proceedings) the term means the scrutiny of the accounts by the Auditor of Court to exclude or amend items unjustifiably included or excessively charged.

Teind. (pr. "teen'd")

Tithe, the tenth part of the annual produce of land, out of which ministers' stipend was originally payable. Also referred to as decimae.

Tenant.

The occupier of a heritable property in terms of a contract of lease constituting a tenancy, the other party to the contract being the landlord. See **Landlord**.

Tender.

An offer made in the course of an action by the defender(s) to the pursuer(s) of a sum in settlement. An example is to be found in an action for damages. If agreement as to the amount of damages cannot be reached, the defender may lodge a tender. If the pursuer accepts the tender, the case is finished; if he rejects it, the case proceeds. If the court eventually awards the pursuer a smaller amount by way of damages than the amount tendered, the pursuer receives only that smaller amount. In those circumstances the defender will also be entitled to his expenses from the date when the pursuer should have accepted the tender.

Tenement.

A building containing a number of separate properties or flats, the body of rules commonly referred to as "the law of tenement" having been evolved to regulate the rights and duties of the proprietors *inter se*. The term is applied sometimes to a piece of land irrespective of whether it is built on. See **Servitude**.

Tenendas.

The clause of tenendas (*tenendas praedictas terras*) expresses the form of feudal tenure by which lands are to be held, e.g. feu farm, i.e. for payment of a *reddendo* in the form of a feuduty. The imposition of feuduties has since 1974 been statutorily prohibited.

Tenor.

See **Proving the tenor**.

Tenure.

(i) The basis on which land is held by one person from another involving in feudal tenure (in its various forms) the relationship of superior and vassal.

(ii) The terms on which a person's appointment or employment is held.

Terce.

The liferent of one-third of her husband's heritage formerly but no longer given by law to a widow who had not accepted a special provision under his will or otherwise discharged her right.

Term.

The date at which rent or interest is payable. Legal terms or term-days are now Whitsunday (May 28) and Martinmas (November 28). In England the word means the duration of a lease and also a session of the Court. See **Whitsunday; Martinmas**.

Tertius.

See **Third party**.

Testament.

Or will: a document whereby a person gives directions for the disposal of his estate on his death. The term is also used in connection with confirmation. Confirmation of an executor nominate being called testament-testamentar and confirmation of an executor dative, testament-dative.

Testate.

As applied to the succession to the estate of a deceased person, described as the testator, signifies the existence of a will or other testamentary document regulating the disposal of his estate. See **Intestacy**.

Test case.

An action brought with a view to determining the law in some matter of common or general application.

Testimony.

Oral evidence given in court under oath.

Testing-clause.

The attestation clause that sets out the execution of a deed, identifying the witnesses and specifying the date and place of execution.

Thing.

An item of property, owned (or capable of being owned) by a person or persons. Things can be divided, for example, into moveable and heritable, corporeal and incorporeal or public or private. Things can be owed or due by one person to another as a result of an obligation. It is the second category of Roman law's tripartite categorisation of law into "persons, things and actions". See **Person; Obligation**.

Third party (otherwise *Tertius*).

A person who although not a party to a relationship or transaction between two others is in some way concerned with or affected by it. See *Jus quaesitum tertio*.

Thirlage.

See **Multures**.

Thole.

To suffer or endure; to *thole an assize* is to undergo a criminal trial, after which no trial on the same charge can take place. See **Res Judicata**.

Tigni immittendi.

One of two Roman law servitudes falling into the category of urban support, the other being *oneris ferendi*. *Tigni immittendi* is the right of the dominant tenement to fix a beam or joist through into the house of the servient tenement for support. See **Servitude**.

Timeous.

An inelegant and unnecessary word meaning in due time, punctual, up to time. Pronounced time-ous, not timmy-ous.

Tinsel.

Forfeiture: usually in the phrase *tinsel of the feu*, incurred for non-payment of feuduty. From *time* or *tyne*, to forfeit.

Title.

The legal basis on which a person has rights to property or other assets the relative documents in the case of land being referred to as "titles" or "title deeds".

Title to exclude.

In an action of reduction this means a title in the defender preferable to that on which the pursuer founds.

Title to sue.

The formal legal right to bring an action. See **Locus standi**.

Titular.

Usually, a person who has the title of teinds, but strictly one with a title to anything.

Tocher. (pr. as in "loch")

The marriage portion or dowry of a wife, common in former times.

Tort.

The English equivalent of **delict**.

***Traditio* (or tradition).**

An expression deriving from Roman law meaning delivery, occasionally used.

Transfer.

The making over, usually voluntarily, of certain rights in property by one party to another, e.g. company shares where the term is applied to the document used. See **Transmission**.

Transference.

The process by which an action is transferred to the representatives of a party to it who has died, or is moved from one court or division of a court to another.

Transmission.

A transfer of rights from one person to another usually involuntarily as by the operation of law on death or bankruptcy. See **Transfer**.

Treasure-trove.

Valuables of which the owner is unknown, found in the ground and assumed to be abandoned (in accordance with the Roman law maxim *quod nullius est, fit domini regis*, meaning "that which is the property of no-one becomes the property of the sovereign"). Treasure-trove belongs to the Crown and in Scotland is administered by the Queen's and Lord Treasurer's Remembrancer.

Trespass.

In the limited sense given to it in Scotland, trespass is any temporary intrusion upon the land of another person without his permission.

Trial.

The hearing of the evidence in a case in civil proceedings with a jury and in criminal proceedings with or without a jury. In a civil matter a hearing before a judge alone is referred to as a proof.

Tribunal.

A person or body of persons other than a court of law, having power to determine claims or disputes of some particular nature.

Truck Acts.

A series of Acts that struck at payment of wages in kind. The Truck Acts have now been repealed. In their place the Wages Act 1986 makes provision for the protection of workers in relation to the payment of wages.

Trust.

The vesting of certain rights or interests in property in certain persons (trustees) to be applied or administered for the benefit of others (beneficiaries) as effected by deed **inter vivos** or *mortis causa* of the truster or by operation of law.

Turpis causa.

Some consideration in a contract that is immoral in the widest sense. See *Contra bonos mores*.

Tutor.

The guardian of children in pupillarity: who could be named by parents (*tutor nominate*); appointed by Court (*tutor dative*); or entitled at law (*tutor-at-law*). See **Pupil**.

U

Uberrimae fidei.

Meaning "of the utmost good faith", being the standard required of parties to certain types of contract including insurance.

Udal tenure. (pr. "ooh-dahl")

Land tenure once common in Orkney and Shetland, but now understood to be rare, by virtue of which the owners hold of the Crown for a payment called skat, but without the usual feudal incidents of Scottish landownership. Since 1974 the imposition by deed of **skat duty** in respect of the tenure or use of land has been prohibited by statute.

Ultimus haeres.

Last heir; the Crown takes as *ultimus haeres* for want of other heirs.

Ultra fines compromissi.

Meaning "beyond the scope of the submission or reference". A decision *ultra fines compromissi* makes the award of a person such as an arbiter liable to partial or total reduction.

Ultra vires.
Meaning "beyond the power" and used generally to signify an act beyond a person's legal authority. More particularly it is the principle applying to public authorities, companies, trustees or others with powers limited by statute or constituting deed, rendering acts or contracts outwith these powers void and incapable of ratification. The principle also applies to delegated legislation such as **bye-laws**.

Ultroneous.
Spontaneous or voluntary.

Umquhile. (pr. "oom-quill")
Former, late, formerly.

Undefended cause or action.
An action in which the defender or defenders have failed to appear to contest.

Underwriter.
(i) The insurer who undertakes to indemnify parties losing by accident at sea.
(ii) A person who agrees to take up any shares not disposed of when a company makes an offer of its shares to the public.

Unfair contract terms.
Certain contractual terms excluding or restricting liability for breach of contract may be void or voidable under the Unfair Contract Terms Act 1977.

Unfair preference.
The giving of a preference by a person aware of his insolvency to one of his creditors to the prejudice of other creditors, challengeable under the Bankruptcy (Scotland) Act 1985 where the preference was created not earlier than six months before the date of sequestration. At common law any transaction by an insolvent debtor conferring a benefit on one creditor in preference to others is challengeable as a **Fraudulent preference; Gratuitous alienation**.

Unico contextu.
In one connection, by one and the same act as part of a continuous process.

Unilateral.
As applied to an act or obligation means that only one person was actively involved, e.g. making a will as contrasted with entering into a contract, which is a bilateral agreement.

Universal successor.
A person or persons succeeding to the totality of the rights and duties of a deceased person, as contrasted with the singular successor such as a purchaser from another person who acquires only one particular item

of property and that free from liabilities in so far as not attaching to that property. See **Succession**.

Universitas.
The whole property of an individual.

Unjustified enrichment.
The legal state where A becomes the owner of B's money or property, or A uses B's property or otherwise benefits from B's actings or expenditure, in circumstances that the law regards as actionably unjust and so requiring the enrichment of A to be reversed. The reversal of the enrichment does not depend on contractual agreement but is obediential, arising by operation of law. Generally, unjustified enrichment may be categorised as:

(i) "**Repetition**", involving recovery of money;

(ii) "**Restitution**", involving recovery of moveable property; and

(iii) "**Recompense**", involving benefit from the expenditure or actings of another or the use of another's propety. The person enriched is described as _lucratus_. The principles of unjustified enrichment are often similarly described as being "quasi-contractual" or as being implied terms of contract law. See **_Lucratus_**; **_Quantum lucratus_**; **_Quantum meruit_**.

Unum quid.
One single thing: applicable where several things are for some purpose to be regarded as one.

Uplift.
To take delivery, usually of money, from a place of custody.

Upset price.
The price at which property is put up for sale by auction, i.e. the price at which bidding begins.

Urban.
Relating to a dwelling-house or other building, rather than in the lay sense of relating to a city, as in _urban lease_ or _urban servitude_.

Usucapio.
In Roman law, the acquisition of property as a result of (among other factors) a specific period of possession. It is similar to modern acquisition by statutory positive prescription.

Usufruct.
See **Liferent**.

Uterine.
Born of the same mother but of different fathers. See **Consanguinean**.

Ut intus.
As within; a reference in one part of a book or document to another part.

Ut supra.

As above.

Utter.

In regard to forgery and coining, to utter is the crime of putting the false writing or coin to the use for which it was meant, whether or not the attempt is successful.

V

Vacant possession.

Refers to the practice whereby heritable property is sold on the basis that the purchaser will receive full and unrestricted possession at the date of entry or settlement.

Vacations.

The periods of the year during which the civil courts are closed for normal business. During these periods the courts function only for urgent or immediate business, the arrangements in the Court of Session involving what is known as the Vacation Court presided over by the Vacation Judge.

Vassal.

In feudal law, the owner of the *dominium utile* of land. He holds the land in the same way as the feudal vassal held of his lord, not as out and out owner, and conditionally on his fulfilling certain conditions and obligations. See **Feu**.

Verbal injury.

Statements that although not defamatory may be actionable, e.g. as holding the person concerned up to public hatred and contempt.

Verdict.

The decision of a jury on the matter or matters submitted to it by the court. In Scottish criminal law, there are three jury verdicts: guilty, not guilty and not proven; the latter two being verdicts of acquittal.

Vergens ad inopiam.

Approaching insolvency, a condition with important legal consequences in relation to the action that creditors of the party so placed may take to protect their interests. See *In meditatione fugae*.

Veritas convicii.

Truth of the insult; a fuller name of the defence to an action of defamation usually summed up as *veritas*.

Verity, Oath of.

An oath of truth. It particularly applied where a creditor petitioned for sequestration of (or claimed in a sequestration against) his debtor. The creditor was required to take an oath as to the truth of his claim.

Vest, To.

To become the property of a person. In succession it signifies the acquisition of a right unaffected by a condition such as survival to a future date. See *Spes Successionis*.

Vexatious litigant.

A person who takes proceedings primarily for the annoyance or embarrassment of the defender and whose activities in raising actions may be restrained by the Court of Session upon application to it made in the name of the **Lord Advocate**. Whether a person is considered a vexatious litigant does not depend simply upon the number of actions he has raised, but includes the manner in which he has conducted himself in the legal process, the taking of a succession of hopeless appeals and abuse of process.

Vicarious liability.

The liability in delict of one person for the acts of another acting on his behalf and under his directions. For example, an employer will be delictually liable for the acts or omissions of an employee in the course of his employment.

View.

An inspection of premises, the subject matter of an action, sometimes allowed to jurors before a jury trial takes place.

Vindicatio.

See **Real action**.

Violent profits.

Penal damages (twice the rent in urban tenancies, in rural the highest profit derivable from the land, together with compensation for any damage caused) due on a tenant's unwarrantable detention of the premises when he should have removed (i.e. when he possesses in **bad faith**).

Vis aut metus.

The Latin term for "force or fear" (and not "force *and* fear" as often wrongly stated). The full brocard is "*vis aut metus qui cadit in constantem virum*" meaning "a force or fear sufficient to overcome a man of firmness and resolution". Such force or fear, if proved, is grounds for the reduction of a contract.

Vitious intromission.

The unwarrantable dealing with moveables of a deceased person, subjecting the offender to potential unlimited liability for the deceased's debts. Where several are concerned in intromission, each is liable *in solidum*.

Vitium reale.

See *Labes realis*.

Voces signatae.

Formal words with a special technical meaning.

Void.

Null, without effect. Any void legal relationship (e.g. a marriage between a brother and sister) is treated as a nullity. See **Voidable**.

Voidable.

Any legal relationship capable of being rendered null or without effect (e.g. in certain circumstances, an unconsummated marriage). A voidable relationship remains valid until:

(i) a party to it rescinds; or

(ii) it is declared void by a court (on the application of a party to the relationship). See **Void**.

Volenti.

A contraction of the maxim "volenti non fit injuria" meaning "no wrong is done to one who consents". The maxim sets out the principle that a person accepting the risk of the injury he has sustained cannot claim civil damages for that injury.

Voucher.

(i) A document acknowledging the payment of money.

(ii) A document to be exchanged for goods or services for which payment has already been made.

W

Wadset.

Now obsolete, it is a conveyance of land by a debtor to his creditor in security of the debt. The debtor (known as the "*reverser*") retains the right of recovery of the land on repayment of the debt. The creditor is referred to as the *wadsetter*. Wadset has been superseded by the statutory standard security.

Waiver.

The renunciation, express or implied, of some right. From feudal law, an example of express renunciation is a minute of waiver granted by a superior cancelling or modifying certain conditions of a **feu**.

Ward.

(i) A term more frequently used in England than in Scotland signifying a person who has a guardian either because of young age or of mental incapacity. See **Nonage; Pupil; Minor**.

(ii) As used in feudal conveyancing the word refers to an obsolete form of feudal tenure known as ward holding by virtue of which the vassal was required to render military services to his superior.

Ward-holding, Charter of.

See **Ward**.

Ware.

Seaweed of various species, also called sea-ware.

Warn.

To notify of the termination of a contract of service or of a lease.

Warrandice.

A clause, usually in a disposition of heritage, by which the granter obliges himself that the right conveyed shall be effectual. This is referred to as *personal warrandice,* and it only binds the granter personally. It is divided into either:

(i) *simple warrandice,* when the granter warrants that he will do nothing inconsistent with the grant (most commonly the form of warrandice in a grant by donation);

(ii) *warrandice from fact and deed,* where the granter warrants that he has not done and will not do any act contrary to the grant; and

(iii) *absolute warrandice (contra omnes mortales),* whereby the granter warrants against any cause of loss. *Real warrandice,* now abolished by statute existed: (a) by force of law on an excambion; and (b) when other land (warrandice lands) were conveyed in security and constituted a security or burden affecting land.

Warrant.

A written authority, e.g. from a court, authorising certain actions such as a search of premises or an eviction of occupiers. Also used to signify a document evidencing a right of some kind, e.g. in a title to heritable property.

Warrant sale.

Now obsolete, this was the public sale by which a creditor who had poinded his debtor's goods disposed of them (the sheriff having granted "warrant" for the sale to proceed). It was formerly typical for the sale to take place in the debtor's home. Under the statutory diligence of **Attachment,** warrant sales are replaced by public auction of a debtor's goods.

Warranty.

A material or essential term of a contract breach of which justifies its termination by the party not at fault. In some contracts such as sale of goods certain warranties (e.g. that the goods will be of satisfactory quality) are implied by law.

Way.

A form of servitude, creating a means of reaching heritable property by crossing that of another. See *Iter.*

Way-going crop.

The crop, ripe at or about the term date of **Martinmas,** which the tenant may usually then take. This was because agricultural tenancies would often terminate at Martinmas.

Wayleave.

A right of way under, across or over land, e.g. for pipelines, cables or wires. While similar in effect to a servitude it is not classed as one, there being strictly no relationship of dominant and servient tenement. See **Servitude**.

White-bonnet.

One who, in collusion with the seller, bids at auction for the purpose of enhancing the price. The intervention of a white-bonnet at auction constitutes a fraud on the other bidders and either the next highest offerer will be preferred to the purchaser, or the sale effected by such means may be entirely set aside.

Whitsunday.

One of the two term days in Scotland (the other being Martinmas) as well as being one of the four quarter days. Whitsunday was formerly May 15 but is now by statute May 28. See **Candlemas; Lammas; Martinmas**.

Wilful.

Intentional or deliberate as opposed to accidental or negligent.

Will.

See **Testament**. The words "at will" as applied to a partnership or tenancy contract signify that it is of no fixed duration but terminable at any time on reasonable notice.

Wind up.

To liquidate, or put an end to the existence of a partnership or a limited company.

Witness.

(i) A person called upon to give evidence in court.

(ii) An instrumentary witness, i.e. a person who signs a document to signify that he saw it signed by a party to it or heard that party acknowledge his signature.

Writ.

This word is mainly used as meaning any writing possessing legal significance, rather than in the narrow English sense of a writ of summons (loose equivalent to a Scottish **Initial writ** or **Summons**).

Writer.

An older name for solicitor, now rather rare. For "Writer to the Signet ('W. S.')" see **Signet**.

Writing.

A document handwritten, typed or printed, as required for certain transactions or contracts in which an oral statement is ineffective.

Y

Yares.
> See **Zares**.

Year and day.
> The lapse of a year has several important effects in the law of Scotland, the day being added to indubitably show that a year has passed. Examples include:
> (i) the calling in court of a summons, which generally must take place within one year of its execution (three months in an action for personal injuries); and
> (ii) the commencement of a criminal trial on indictment must happen within one year of the accused person's first appearance on petition.

Year to year.
> The description of a contract such as tenancy that continues indefinitely but is terminable on due notice at the end of any yearly period.

Young person.
> A person aged over 16 and under 21 who is found guilty of a crime may be subject to punishment but not to imprisonment. By statute young persons may be sentenced to detention in a Young Offenders Institution.

Z

Zares, Zaires, Yares or **Yairs.** (pr. "yerz")
> Forms of enclosures made for the purposes of fishing in watercourses: permissible for white fish but no longer in use for salmon.

COMMON LEGAL ACRONYMS
AND
ABBREVIATIONS

A.C.	Appeal Cases (Law Reports).
A.P.S.	Acts of the Parliament of Scotland 1424–1707.
asp	Acts of the Scottish Parliament 1999–.
Act of Adj.	Act of Adjournal.
Act of Sed.	Act of Sederunt.
All E.R.	All England Law Reports.
All E.R. (Comm)	All England Law Reports Commercial Cases.
All E.R. (EC)	All England Law Reports European Cases.
art.	article.
B. & Ad.	Barnewall and Adolphus's Reports (King's Bench, England).
B. & Ald.	Barnewall and Alderson's Reports (King's Bench, England).
B. & C.	Barnewall and Cresswell's Reports (King's Bench, England).
BCC	British Company Cases.
B.C.L.C.	Butterworths Company Law Cases.
B.T.LC.	Butterworths Trading Law Cases.
B. & S.	Best and Smith's Reports (Queen's Bench, England).
B.Y.I.L.	British Yearbook of International Law.
Bell. App.	Bell's Scotch Appeals (House of Lords).
Brown's Supp.	Brown's Supplement to Morison's Dictionary of Decisions.
c.	chapter (of an Act of Parliament).
CA	Court of Appeal (England & Wales).
C.A.R.	Criminal Appeal Reports.
C.B.	Common Bench (England).
C.B.N.S.	Common Bench New Series (England).
CCR	County Court Rules (England).
CJEC	Court of Justice of the European Communities.
C.L.	Current Law Monthly Digest.
C.L.C.	Commercial Law Cases.
C.L.J.	Current Law Journal.
C.L.P.	Current Legal Problems.
C.L.Q.	Current Law Quarterly.
C.L.R.	Commonwealth Law Reports.
C.L.Y.	Current Law Yearbook.
CMAC	Courts-Martial Appeal Court.
C.M.L.R.	Common Market Law Reports.
Ch D	Chancery Division (Law Reports).
Cl. & Fin.	Clark and Finnelly's Reports (House of Lords)

Co. Rep.	Coke's Reports.
Cox C.C.	Cox's Criminal Cases.
CSIH	Court of Session Inner House (decisions).
CSOH	Court of Session Outer House (decisions).
D.	Dunlop's Session Cases.
DC	Divisional Court (England & Wales).
D.L.R.	Dominion Law Reports (Canada).
EAT	Employment Appeal Tribunal.
E. & B.	Ellis and Blackburn's Reports (Queen's Bench, England).
E. & E.	Ellis and Ellis's Reports (Queen's Bench, England).
EC	European Communities.
E.C.C.	European Commercial Cases.
ECJ	European Court of Justice.
E.C.R.	European Court Reports (Court of Justice of the European Communities).
ECSC	European Coal and Steel Community.
EEC	European Economic Community.
E.H.R.R.	European Human Rights Reports.
E.L.R.	Edinburgh Law Review.
E.R.	English Reports.
EWCA	England and Wales Court of Appeal.
Exch.	Exchequer Division (Law Reports).
F.	Fraser's Session Cases.
F.C.	Faculty Collection.
Fam Div	Family Division (Law Reports).
G.W.D.	Greens Weekly Digest.
HCJ	High Court of Justiciary (decisions, first instance).
HCJAC	High Court of Justiciary Appeal Court (decisions).
HL	House of Lords.
HL Cas.	House of Lords Cases.
H.L.R.	Harvard Law Review/Housing Law Reports.
Hume.	Hume's Decisions (Court of Session).
I.C.L.Q.	International and Comparative Law Quarterly.
I.C.R.	Industrial Case Reports.
I.H.	Inner House (Court of Session).
I.P.D.	*In Praesenti Dominorum* (in the presence of their Lordships; found on Inner House Interlocutors).
I.R.L.R.	Industrial Relations Law Reports.
I.T.R.	Industrial Tribunal Reports.
Irv.	Irvine's Justiciary Reports.
J.	Justice (i.e. a Judge of the High Court of England & Wales or N. Ireland).
JJ.	Justices (plural of J. above).
J.C.	Justiciary Cases (reported within Session Cases).
J.L.H.	Journal of Legal History.
JLSS	Journal of the Law Society of Scotland.

J.R.	Juridical Review (Scotland).
K.B.	Kings Bench Division (Law Reports).
K.I.R.	Knights Industrial Reports.
L.C.	Lord Chancellor (England & Wales).
L.J.	Lord Justice (Judge of the Court of Appeal of England & Wales or N. Ireland).
L.JJ.	Lords Justices (plural of L.J. above).
L.J.R.	Law Journal Reports.
L.Q.R.	Law Quarterly Review.
L.R.	Law Reports (England & Wales).
L.T.	Law Times Reports (England).
L.V.A.C.	Land Valuation Appeal Court (Scotland).
Law Com.	Law Commission (England).
Lloyds Rep.	Lloyd's List Law Reports.
M.	Macpherson's Session Cases.
M.R.	Master of the Rolls (England & Wales).
M. & W.	Meeson and Welsby's Reports (England).
Mac. & G.	Macnaughten and Gordon's Reports (England).
Macq.	Macqueen's House of Lords Reports.
Mor.	Morison's Dictionary of Decisions (Court of Session).
N.I.	Northern Ireland Reports.
N.I.L.Q.	Northern Ireland Law Quarterly.
N.L.J.	New Law Journal.
N.W.T.R.	North West Territories Reports.
OED	Oxford English Dictionary.
O.H.	Outer House (Court of Session).
OJ	Official Journal of the European Communities.
Ont. C.A.	Ontario Court of Appeal (Canada).
P.	Probate, Divorce and Admiralty Division (Law Reports).
PC	Privy Council (Judicial Committee).
P.I.Q.R.	Personal Injuries and Quantum Reports.
P. & M.I.L.L.	The Personal and Medical Injuries Law Letter.
Pat.	Paton's House of Lords Appeal Cases.
Q.B.	Queen's Bench (Law Reports).
R.	Rettie's Session Cases.
R.P.C.	Reports of Patents, Designs and Trade Marks Cases.
R.T.R.	Road Traffic Reports.
Rep. B.	Reparation Bulletin.
Rep. L.R.	Reparation Law Reports.
Robin.	Robinson's Scotch Appeals (House of Lords).
S.	Shaw's Session Cases.
s.	section (of an Act of Parliament).
S.A.	South African Law Reports (1947–)
S.A.L.R.	South African Law Reports
S.C.	Session Cases.

S.C.A.	Scottish Court Administration.
S.C.C.R.	Scottish Criminal Case Reports.
S.C.C.R.Supp.	Scottish Criminal Case Reports Supplement (1950–1980).
S.C. (HL)	Session Cases (House of Lords).
S.C. (J.)	High Court of Justiciary Cases (reported within Session Cases volumes).
S.C.L.R.	Scottish Civil Law Reports.
SCOLAG	Scottish Legal Action Group.
S.C.S.S.	Scottish Council of Social Service.
S.H.L.R.	Scottish Housing Law Reports.
SI	Statutory Instrument.
S.J.	Scottish Jurist.
S.L.C.R.	Scottish Land Court Reports.
S.L.G.	Scottish Law Gazette.
S.L.R.	Scottish Law Reporter.
S.L.T.	Scots Law Times.
S.L.T. (Notes)	Scots Law Times Notes of Recent Decisions.
S.L.T. (Sh. Ct.)	Scots Law Times Sheriff Court Reports.
S.N.	Session Notes.
S.P.L.P.	Scottish Planning Law and Practice.
SR & O	Statutory Rules and Orders.
SSI.	Scottish Statutory Instrument.
Scot. Law. Com.	Scottish Law Commission.
Shaw App.	Shaw's Scotch Appeals (House of Lords).
Sol. J.	Solicitors' Journal.
T.L.R.	Times Law Reports.
W.L.R.	Weekly Law Reports.
W.N.	Weekly Notes (Law Reports).
W.R.	Weekly Reporter (England).
W. & S.	Wilson and Shaw's House of Lords Cases.
W.W.R.	Western Weekly Reports (Canada).
Y.E.L.	Yearbook of European Law.
Yale .L.J.	Yale Law Journal.

LEGAL AND RELATED WEBSITES

British and Irish Legal Information Institute: Searchable databases of UK, Irish and European case law and statutes, and other resources, including links to free legal resources worldwide.
http://www.bailii.org [Accessed February 17, 2009].

McBain's Dictionary: Includes a searchable dictionary of the Gaelic language.
http://www.ceantar.org [Accessed February 17, 2009].

Office of Public Sector Information: Includes UK Acts, Acts of the Scottish Parliament, Northern Irish and Welsh Assemblies, statutory instruments and Measures of the General Synod of the Church of England.
http://www.opsi.gov.uk [Accessed February 17, 2009].

Privy Council Office: Includes decisions of the Judicial Committee of the Privy Council.
http://www.privy-council.org.uk [Accessed February 17, 2009].

Scottish Courts: Information about Scotland's courts (including the location and contact details for Sheriff Courts, the Court of Session and the High Court of Justiciary) as well as written decisions.
http://www.scotcourts.gov.uk [Accessed February 17, 2009].

Scots Law Resources: Includes a variety of useful links to courts, legislation, journals, government websites, and other organisations and professional bodies.
http://www.scottishlaw.org.uk [Accessed February 17, 2009].

Scottish Government:
http://www.scotland.gov.uk [Accessed February 17, 2009].

Scottish Land Court: Includes decisions of the Scottish Land Court and the Lands Tribunal for Scotland.
http://www.scottish-land-court.org.uk [Accessed February 17, 2009].

Scottish Law Commission:
http://www.scotlawcom.gov.uk [Accessed February 17, 2009].

Scottish Parliament:
http://www.scottish.parliament.uk [Accessed February 17, 2009].

United Kingdom Government:
http://www.direct.gov.uk [Accessed February 17, 2009].

United Kingdom Parliament: Includes information about Bills before Parliament and matters before the Judicial Committee of the House of Lords.
http://www.parliament.uk [Accessed February 17, 2009].